Acknowledgements

I would like to sincerely thank my wife Margot and daughter Meagan who have made it possible for me to write this book. Their willingness to sacrifice their own time and too much of our time as a family were instrumental in helping this project reach completion. Meagan, your editing and proofreading talents are so greatly appreciated (despite your sometimes brutal treatment of my attempts at narrative). Margot, your humour, personal resolve and physical strength continue to impress and amaze me.

For their support (and tolerance), many thanks to my colleagues at Maritime Physiotherapy, especially Robert MacDonald, David MacDonald and Sarah Gordon, and of course the many patients and conditioning clients whose motivation and willingness to try something new provided me with an ongoing source of confidence in this project. Thanks specifically to Bep, Bruce, Debbie, Maggie, Chris, Anne Marie and Maryn for your contributions to this book.

For their inspiration and demonstration of what it is to be a professional, a clinician and an educator, my thanks to Anne Augur, Sharon Shafir and Molly Verrier at the University of Toronto.

For their inspiration and demonstration of what it is to be a friend, my everlasting gratitude to Mike Drinkwater, Nola and Mathew Hart, Rob MacDonald and Evelyn Sutton, Christa MacKinnon and Simon Roberts. A special thanks also to Rob Dewitt in Halifax for reminding me that this was a book worth writing!

Finally, a book of this type could not be conceived of let alone written for 'public consumption' without the scientific research conducted by various professionals from around the world. I would like to single out the following for their substantial contributions to the rehabilitation of people who have orthopaedic pathology: Manohar Panjabi, Carolyn Richardson, Paul Hodges, Gwen Jull, Julie Hides, Diane Lee, Moshe Solomonow and Stuart McGill. My ability to effectively treat people with spinal conditions has been enhanced tremendously thanks to the research and clinical models generated by these individuals. This book is merely a reconstruction of their work in a language I hope the non-medical professional can understand.

Rick Jemmett

Contents ...

Preface

The second edition of *Spinal Stabilization - The New Science of Back Pain* has been updated and expanded for two important reasons. Since writing the first edition, new scientific studies of the Australian spinal stabilization method have been published. This research has provided us with a better appreciation for the extent to which therapeutic stabilization exercises can lower a person's risk of future low back pain episodes.

The second reason was a recognition of the need to clarify the important distinctions between stabilization exercises utilized for therapeutic purposes and those used for sport conditioning purposes. There are fundamental differences between stabilization exercises that will help correct the underlying problems associated with low back pain and those which will provide athletes with a more well trained trunk or core. I realized that this book could be re-structured to better explain these differences and thus help readers make more informed exercise selections.

A primary goal of the first edition was to incorporate, in a single book, a full spectrum of stabilization exercises. These ranged from specific techniques intended to correct the unique pathology-related problems of people with low back pain to highly challenging exercises designed to improve athletic performance. The exercises were presented in a simple framework intended to provide non-health care professionals with an easy appreciation for this rather complex topic. At the same time, I had hoped that health care professionals would be able to use the book as a flexible resource complementing their personal approach to the treatment of low back pain.

While these goals remain unchanged, I felt it was important to more directly address the distinctions between therapeutic and conditioning-related stabilization training. For these reasons, the second edition of *Spinal Stabilization - The New Science of Back Pain* has been rewritten in some significant ways.

The book is now divided into two primary sections, Book I and Book II. The first is concerned with the injured spine, while the second deals with the healthy spine. If you have a low back problem of any kind, you should begin with Book I. At the same time, seek out a health care professional skilled in the Australian method of segmental spinal stabilization to help you. When you have mastered the exercises in Book I, your back pain should be well under control. You may then progress to the exercises in Book II if you wish to develop greater strength and power in your core muscles.

If you have a healthy spine and you have not had a significant episode of low back pain in several years, you might choose to read chapters one and two and then proceed to the exercises in Book II, chapter six.

Welcome to the second edition of *Spinal Stabilization - The New Science of Back Pain*. I hope this book remains both a valuable asset to those with low back pain and a challenging approach to core conditioning for people fortunate enough to have a healthy spine.

Introduction

This is a book for people like you who have a back.

It is a book for people who have back pain and for people who would rather avoid the experience of back pain altogether. It is a book for people - nurses, parents and lawyers, butchers, bakers and software makers - who need a healthy back to do their jobs and perform their everyday activities. It is a book for people who run, ride, swim or skate; people who throw things, swing things, paddle things or kick things - a book for people who want to avoid injury and improve their athletic performance.

Spinal stabilization is a new concept in rehabilitation and sports conditioning based on recent research regarding our spine and its supporting muscles. This research has led to a more comprehensive understanding of how our back is intended to work. It has also provided us with greater insight into spinal pathology and the causes of low back pain. With this new appreciation for the healthy and the injured spine, physical therapists in Australia and Canada have developed a unique approach to the treatment of low back pain. This new, research-proven approach is already being used by enlightened physical therapists and other health care professionals around the world. Many strength training experts have borrowed and extended these new concepts to improve the physical conditioning programs of professional and national-level athletes.

Spinal Stabilization ...

Traditionally, rehabilitation professionals have felt that in order to have a healthy back, a person must have strong abdominal and spinal muscles. To that end, physical therapists and doctors have long prescribed various strength-based programs for their patients with back pain. Unfortunately, according to more recent research, few patients realized any significant long-term improvement in their symptoms using sit-ups and back strengthening exercises. In fact, some people noted that their back and neck pain became worse as they performed such exercises. Many more people would continue to have episodes of back pain despite continuing with their home exercise programs.

As it turned out, rehabilitation professionals didn't yet have enough information regarding the detailed workings of the spine to design consistently successful therapeutic exercise programs for people with back or spinal pathology.

Similarly, coaches and athletes have long relied on the abdominal and back strengthening exercises which originated in the world of body-building. While these exercises are useful in developing the large, power generating muscles of the trunk, they do little to train the deeper muscles of the abdomen and back. These deep spinal muscles, sometimes referred to as *core* muscles, are essential to optimal performance in virtually every sport. In fact, they are critical to ideal spinal function in all activities.

The New Science of Back Pain ...

Over the past few years, researchers in the United States, Australia, Europe, Canada and Japan have shed new light on the way our spine works. The spinal stabilization approach discussed in Book I is based on a dramatically improved understanding of the function of the spinal column and its muscles.

We now know that the various muscles of the spine serve very different purposes. Some act as position sensors, some act as stabilizers and others work to create powerful movements. With this improved understanding of spinal function, we have been able to develop more effective exercise prescriptions which train the various trunk muscles for their specific functions.

While the majority of people with back pain will benefit tremendously from the Australian spinal stabilization method, not all of the exercises described in this book are appropriate for everyone. Different people with different back problems at different points in their recovery process will be best served by a program designed for their specific circumstances. Therefore, if you have back pain, you are strongly encouraged to consult a health care professional who uses this approach in their daily practice. He will be able to select the safest and most effective combination of exercises for you and your back problem.

Recreational or competitive athletes who would like a more high-performance, injury-resistant spine, will also find plenty to work with in this book. In fact, the more advanced exercises in Book II will challenge even Olympic-caliber athletes. Although, as an athlete, you may not have selected this book to solve a back pain problem, consultation with a health care professional may still be beneficial in terms of selecting the most appropriate exercises for your sport. She will ensure that you are using proper technique and thus getting the most out of your training program.

The How and Why of Spinal Stabilization

In our daily work with patients and athletes, physical therapists have learned that people are most likely to continue with their exercises if they understand both the how and why of their rehabilitation program.

'Why' refers to why it is that their back hurts and 'how' refers to how the Australian method of spinal stabilization will help them. In order to understand both back injury and the role of the spine in athletic performance, one must first have a basic understanding of how the spine is built and how it works. Therefore, we will begin in chapters one and two with a look at the healthy spine. We'll discover how our spine is intended to work and how our trunk is put together - the function and the anatomy of the trunk and the spinal column. Both athletes and people with low back pain should read these chapters for an overview of proper spinal function.

Chapters three to five in Book I discuss important issues related to low back pain such as how the spine is injured, the meaning of medical diagnostic terminology and most importantly, how to correctly perform the therapeutic spinal stabilization exercises.

For example, chapter four reviews the medical terminology used to define different types of back problems. Diagnostic terms like 'spondylolisthesis', 'sciatica' and 'degenerative disc disease' will be explained in everyday language helping you to better understand your back problem. Chapter four will also discuss the extent to which therapeutic stabilization can be expected to benefit people with different back problems.

Chapter five describes in detail the therapeutic spinal stabilization approach developed by Australian physiotherapists Carolyn Richardson, Julie Hides, Paul Hodges and Gwen Jull. This section will provide you with the most current information available regarding this innovative and scientifically proven method of back pain rehabilitation. Careful attention to the correct performance of these gentle, muscle-isolating exercises has been shown to dramatically lower a person's risk of experiencing ongoing episodes of low back pain.

Book II details the use of stabilization-based conditioning programs for people whose exercise goals are related to fitness or sports. The exercises in Book II are an extension of the 'outer unit' concept developed by Canadian physiotherapist Diane Lee along with spine researcher Dr. Andry Vleeming. A review of the various concepts which provide the foundation for a stabilization-based training program is presented.

Book II will teach you how to apply the principles of spinal stabilization in fitness or sport conditioning situations. Pictures and descriptions of all the exercises are included in these sections. You will learn how to do the exercises correctly and how to progress safely to more advanced variations. These chapters discuss the role of stabilization-based exercises in back injury prevention programs, and the ability of stabilization training to improve athletic performance.

Finally, a collection of spinal stabilization success stories are found in chapter eleven. Here, actual patients describe in their own words their experiences with back pain and how therapeutic and conditioning-based stabilization training helped them reach their back health and fitness goals.

Thank You!

Thank you for choosing this book and congratulations on taking the first step toward incorporating spinal stabilization exercises into your daily routine. Please read all of the text before beginning the exercises, especially if you have low back pain or if you have had back pain within the past few years. Again, if you have a back problem, please see a licensed health care professional familiar with the Australian treatment approach who can help you with your exercises, especially in the early stages. At all times use caution and care recognizing that, as with any exercise program, exercises done correctly will be more safe and effective than exercises done without attention to optimal technique.

If you have any kind of back pain, any neck, shoulder, hip or knee problems, balance disorders or any other medical condition which could possibly be made worse with exercise, you must consult with a physician, physical therapist or chiropractor before attempting these exercises.

Book I

Chapter 1
The Healthy Spine

For years health care professionals had assumed that the human spine was a strong and mechanically sound structure. As far back as the mid-1940's, medical papers described our spinal column - the spinal vertebrae (bones), discs and ligaments - as being sufficiently strong to handle the stresses and strains associated with everyday life. Doctors felt that so long as a person's spinal x-ray looked normal, the spinal column could be considered to be healthy. Based on that assumption, it was felt that typical low back pain was most often due to a muscular injury. However, the diagnosis of muscular back pain was rarely based on any *evidence* of muscular injury, but rather a *lack of evidence* of spinal column injury.

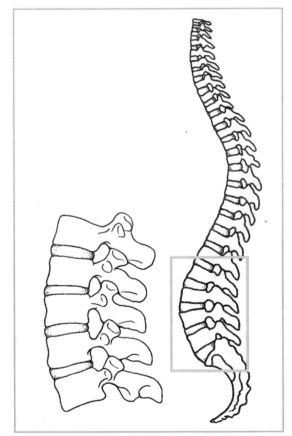

The spinal column and, in more detail, the five vertebrae of the lumbar spine as seen from the left side.

These assumptions persisted for quite some time. Even as recently as the late 1970's, research articles reported that the spinal column (the vertebrae, disc and ligaments) was, by itself, a stable structure. Then a funny thing happened in the world of spinal research.

Someone happened across a lab report written in 1961 by two undergraduate students at the University of California. The students had decided to determine how much stress a normal human spinal column could withstand before becoming injured. Their findings were completely at odds with decades of medical dogma. Instead of being strong enough to handle the majority of the stresses associated with walking, bending, lifting, climbing out of a car, and playing various sports, the human spinal column was exceptionally fragile.

By 1990, new research had shown that while normal everyday activities might place stresses of approximately eighty kilograms (175 lb) on our spine, the strongest region of the spine could tolerate only nine kilograms (20 lb) of stress before buckling under the load and becoming injured. Even more incredible, the stresses on the spine associated with sports such as competitive weightlifting can reach 1600 kilograms. Obviously, the fragile spine itself was not sufficiently stable to provide us with our 'trunk stability'.

Researchers and health care professionals quickly realized that our spinal column was desperately in need of muscular support during even the most basic of activities. Furthermore, if muscles were necessary for spinal support or stability, our neurologic system must also play a key role in spinal stabilization, as our muscles must be controlled by the nervous system in order to function.

Form & Function: The Healthy Spine in Motion

Our spinal column is a series of twenty-five individual bones called vertebrae which are connected by soft tissues known as ligaments and spinal discs. The discs and ligaments attach one vertebrae to the next and, to a degree, limit the small amount of motion that occurs between the vertebrae whenever we move. The upper section of the column, commonly known as the neck, is the cervical spine. The middle region is the thoracic spine and the lowest region is the lumbar spine.

Each pair of vertebrae, for example the fourth and fifth lumbar vertebrae, along with the disc sandwiched between them and the ligaments surrounding them, form what is called a spinal joint.

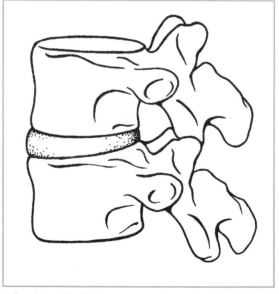

A lumbar spinal joint, as seen from the left. Between the two vertebrae is the spinal disc. Spinal ligaments surround the joint but are not included in these pictures for the sake of clarity.

Not unlike your knee or elbow joint, a spinal joint is where the movements of the spinal column actually occur. The linking of twenty-five vertebrae by the discs and ligaments produces a continuous, flexible column of spinal joints allowing our bodies the freedom to move in many ways.

Throughout the spinal column, motion at single spinal joints comes in two varieties - slides and tilts. The bending movements of our spine result from the sliding and tilting motions occurring at these spinal joints. For example, when you bend forward to tie your shoes, the fourth lumbar vertebrae will both slide a little and tilt a little in the forward direction. When this happens throughout the spinal column, you can bend all the way to the floor.

Large movements of the spine such as bending forward to pick up a golf ball or twisting and reaching into the back seat of the car are the result of small amounts of motion occurring at many spinal joints. Movement at just one or two spinal joints will occur when we are walking or simply reaching an arm across the dinner table for a wine glass. All movements of the body result in some degree of motion at our spinal joints.

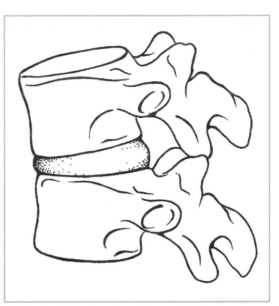

This spinal joint has bent forward with the top vertebrae both sliding and tilting forward a little. The disc is compressed in front and stretched at the back.

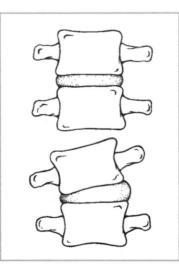

This is a spinal joint, seen from the front. The top drawing shows the joint as it would be with its owner standing straight. The bottom drawing shows the slight slide and tilt that occurs as the person bends to the right side.

Spinal Stability - The Key to Healthy Movement

A healthy spinal column is a very mobile but a relatively weak structure. The vertebrae, like all bones in the body, are strong. However, the discs and ligaments that link neighboring vertebrae together are fairly fragile. The discs and ligaments are the 'weak link' in the spinal column chain, tolerating only six to nine kilograms of stress before an injury occurs. This means that the spinal column itself is unable to support even our own body weight without collapsing. Without muscle, the spinal column will not remain stable.

Before we discuss the important stabilizing effects of spinal muscles, we need to be certain that the concept of spinal joint stability is clearly understood. All joints in the body, as with any other joint such as a door hinge, must remain properly aligned for the joint to work correctly. In the spine, joint stability refers to the extent to which a joint is able to move fully but not excessively. Whether we are discussing a spinal joint, a shoulder joint, or a door hinge, a correct fit must be maintained in order for the joint to move properly and without abnormal wear and tear. In the case of a door hinge, stability is dependent only on the screws which anchor the hinge to the edge of the door. In our spine, stability is much more complicated.

A Dog on a Leash

When we bend forward to tie our shoes or reach overhead to change a light bulb, a small amount of motion occurs at individual spinal joints. The upper vertebrae in the spinal joint slides and tilts a little relative to the bottom vertebrae of the joint. As this motion begins, the disc and ligaments remain relaxed and permit some amount of 'free' motion to occur. In this way the spinal joint behaves like a dog on a leash. The disc and ligaments (the leash) allow the vertebrae (the dog) to move relatively freely, as long as it doesn't move too far, just like your dog is free to move so long as he doesn't stray too far from you.

As the vertebrae moves further the initial 'slack' in the disc and ligaments is taken up. They become tight and, to some extent, prevent the vertebrae from moving further. Notice that I wrote 'to some extent' regarding the ability of the disc and ligaments to prevent further motion of the vertebrae. This is because the disc and ligaments become injured if they are strained by more than nine kilograms of load. They can provide some stability, but not a lot.

Normal daily activities can place several hundred pounds of stress on spinal joints. While the disc and ligaments are important structures of the spine, they are definitely a very weak 'leash'. A spinal joint therefore needs additional support from muscles to control joint motion and prevent injury of the disc or ligaments. If stressed or challenged by more than twenty pounds of force spinal discs and ligaments will be damaged. If injured, the disc and ligaments will allow abnormally large amounts of motion to occur at the spinal joint, just as a torn leash allows a dog to run uncontrolled. Muscle is therefore critical in terms of maintaining healthy spinal stability.

Spinal Stability Muscles vs Spinal Movement Muscles

The idea that muscles are important in keeping the back healthy is not new. Rehabilitation experts have long prescribed back and abdominal strengthening exercises for people with low back problems. One unique feature of our current understanding of the spine is the realization that spinal muscles come in two distinct varieties: stabilizers and movers. Our trunk has certain muscles which stabilize the spinal joints by controlling and limiting spinal joint motion, and certain muscles which create movement of the spinal column as a whole.

Stabilizing muscles tend to be found in the middle layer of the trunk and are relatively short muscles crossing only one or two spinal levels. This arrangement allows middle layer muscles to control the small sliding and tilting motions that occur at spinal joints. Middle layer muscles are therefore designed specifically to prevent disc or ligament injuries and any subsequent development of excess joint motion. We'll look at the deep, middle and outer layers of the trunk in more detail in the next chapter.

Movement muscles form the outer layer of our trunk and are much longer and thicker than stabilizing muscles. These muscles can span up to ten spinal joints without attaching to any of the lumbar vertebrae. As such, they are designed to create large movements of the spinal column and to control the overall posture of the spine. The outer layer muscles also tend to be the power generating muscles of the abdomen and lower back. These are the muscles we use to do a sit-up, to straighten up after bending over, or to lift heavy objects. These are not, however, muscles which require rehabilitation once we have a back problem.

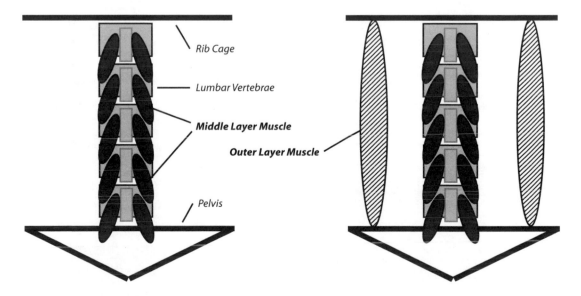

A schematic depiction of the lumbar spine's middle and outer layer muscles. A highly simplified rib cage and pelvis are represented by a horizontal line and a triangle respectively. Middle layer muscles attach vertebrae to vertebrae. The spine on the right shows how outer layer muscles span the pelvis to the ribs without direct attachment to the lumbar vertebrae.

To this point, I've covered two thirds of the important research regarding spinal stabilization. The last third is likely the most important. Without this last bit of information, rehabilitation professionals would still be prescribing generic abdominal and back strengthening exercises for patients with low back pain. This critical factor regarding the stability of our spinal joints concerns the complex process of muscular control.

The Nervous System & Muscular Control

Despite the power of today's computer technologies, robotics researchers remain unable to design systems and software programs capable of controlling the most basic walking movements of a life-sized, fully-jointed robot. A robot the size of an average person and built with the same number of joints will consistently topple over when it attempts to walk a straight line across a level floor. There are simply too many joints with too much potential movement for the computer to control them all and have the robot walk 'normally'.

To produce the infinite number of movements of which people are capable, the muscles of our spine and limbs must be controlled by our 'computer', the central nervous system. Nerves carrying electrical signals to the muscles of the body cause the muscles to activate, or contract, in very specific ways. As we walk, lift things, throw baseballs or ski a mogul run, even as we roll over in bed while sleeping, the nervous system constantly controls the trunk's muscles to maintain stability at our spinal joints. Without ideal control via the nervous system, muscles will fail to work satisfactorily. If the specific muscles responsible for joint stability fail to work correctly, the joint may be injured.

In order to properly control our spinal muscles and maintain spinal joint stability, the nervous system needs to be aware of even the most subtle changes in spinal joint position. This sub-conscious 'position sense' is a critical part of the automatic control of all our movements. To develop this sub-conscious awareness of spinal movement, nerve endings found in the spinal discs and ligaments (the *deep layer* of the spine) send information to the nervous system regarding the position of individual spinal joints. Using this 'position-sense' information, the nervous system can make the ongoing adjustments in muscle tension which are necessary to stabilize and protect our joints, discs and ligaments. Recent research strongly suggests that if the nervous system is deprived of this position-sense information, it will lose the ability to activate certain middle layer muscles, muscles which protect and stabilize the joints of the spinal column.

Low Back Pain, The Nervous System & Muscular Control

To illustrate the concept of normal and faulty muscular control, we can think of the individual muscles of the trunk as being similar to the individual cylinders in a 1970's-vintage sports car with a V-12 engine. In older cars, the ignition wire carried an electrical signal to a distributor cap, which in turn sent the signal to the engine's cylinders, along a wire specific to each cylinder. Similarly, each muscle in our trunk is controlled by a specific nerve which carries an electrical signal from the nervous system to the muscle. In the car engine, if the wire to a specific cylinder was unable to deliver current, that cylinder would not fire, regardless of how hard the driver stepped on the gas. Likewise, if the nervous system fails to signal a given muscle, the muscle will simply not activate normally.

As it turns out, people with low back pain consistently lose some degree of nervous system control of important spinal column muscles. Researchers have found that people with virtually any form of low back pain will develop a neurological inability to 'signal' the key middle layer muscles that stabilize and protect their spinal joints. Therefore, once almost any form of spinal pathology develops, our nervous system is unable to exert optimal control over certain spinal muscles - spinal muscles which are critical to maintaining spinal stability.

If any part of the spinal joint is injured or experiences even the slow, wear and tear types of problems seen with the 'older spine', two different deficits develop. First, the mechanical stabilizing ability of the disc or ligament will diminish, allowing more motion to occur at the spinal joint. In other words, the problematic disc or ligament becomes a longer 'leash' and allows too much movement of the vertebrae.

Second, and even more importantly, once injury or wear and tear affects the disc or ligaments, the positional information these structures normally generate becomes faulty. Unfortunately, our nervous system is very dependent on this positional information to signal or activate the middle layer muscles.

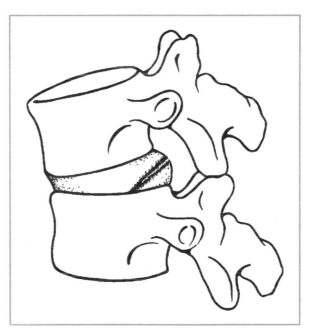

A disc injury will permit excessive motion to develop at a spinal joint. The torn region of the disc will not generate accurate positional information. This becomes an unstable spinal joint as a result of these deficits.

Thus, once a disc, ligament or other spinal joint component becomes pathologic, the nervous system will be without much of the critical 'position-sense' information it requires to optimally control the muscles which protect the spinal joint.

The end result is a simultaneous increase in spinal joint motion (a mechanical problem) along with an impairment of middle layer muscular control (a neurologic problem). This combination of mechanical and neurologic problems is the basis for what we now refer to as a *clinical spinal instability*.

Low Back Pain as a Neurologic Problem

The discovery that low back pain consistently results in diminished neurologic control of protective spinal muscles has led to a huge paradigm shift amongst health care professionals and researchers. The traditional idea of low back pain assumed that the nervous system worked correctly. This, in part, led to the idea that simple muscle strengthening exercises could be used to correct the problem. Now, with our understanding of the neurologic impairment common to low back pain, comes the realization that strengthening exercises of any kind will fail to truly correct the problem.

Earlier the muscles of the trunk were compared to the cylinders in a car's engine. If the wire to a specific cylinder is frayed, the cylinder won't receive a signal. Stepping harder on the gas will only cause the other cylinders, the ones working correctly, to work harder. Likewise, a muscle without proper neurologic input will not suddenly spring to action just because we 'step on the gas', i.e., perform a strengthening exercise. Indeed, in people with low back pain, strength exercises actually overwhelm the nervous system's ability to activate important spine-protective middle-layer muscles.

The next chapter will describe our spinal anatomy in a little more detail and at the same time, review the functions we have just discussed in the context of the deep, middle and outer layers of the trunk.

Chapter 2
Anatomy of the Stable Spine

When teaching patients about how their back is built and how it works, I have found it helpful to describe the back as a structure consisting of three layers. These three layers - the deep, middle and outer layers - have specific roles to play in maintaining a healthy, stable spine.

The Deep Layer

The deep layer consists primarily of the spinal joints of the spinal column - the vertebrae, discs and ligaments - and a series of small muscles running from one vertebrae to the next. The discs and ligaments perform two functions: helping to stabilize the spine (mechanical function) and providing the brain with information about the exact position of every spinal joint (neurological function). The tiny muscles found in the deep layer also generate this positional information.

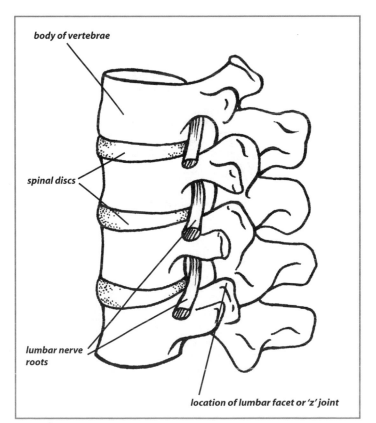

body of vertebrae

spinal discs

lumbar nerve roots

location of lumbar facet or 'z' joint

Four of the five lumbar vertebrae shown from the left side.

The Middle Layer

Four key muscles of the middle layer provide the bulk of the stability required to keep our lower back working effectively and without pain. Two are back muscles and one is an abdominal muscle. The stabilizing muscles which are found in the back are the multifidus and the quadratus lumborum. The primary spine stabilizer from the abdominal group is the transversus abdominis.

A fourth muscle of the middle layer, the psoas (pronounced, 'so-as'), may also play an important role in spinal stabilization. At this time less is known about the psoas as a stabilizer although emerging research suggests that it may be just as important as the three muscles mentioned above.

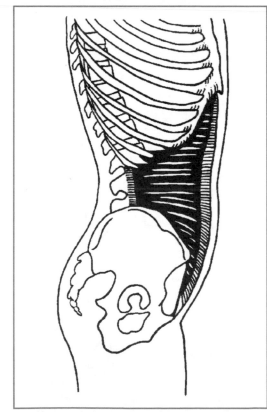

Transversus Abdominus - a middle layer stabilizing muscle, shown from the right side

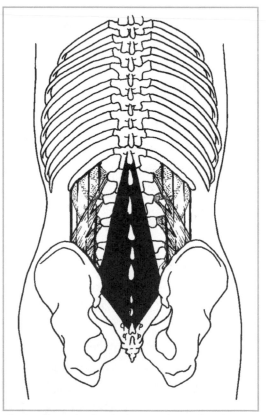

Shown from the back, the quadratus lumborum and multifidus muscles - multifidus is the more central of these muscles

The Outer Layer

This is the layer of thick, long muscles which are found just below the skin. These muscles provide the power necessary to straighten up from a bent position, swing a baseball bat or a golf club or to lift heavy objects. The outer layer muscles of the back are collectively known as the erector spinae muscles. The three remaining abdominal muscles, the external oblique, internal oblique and the rectus abdominis (the 'six-pack') are also components of this final layer.

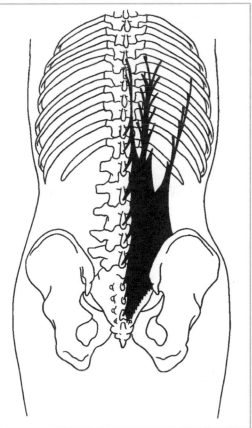

The erector spinae muscle, seen from behind. The primary outer layer muscle of the back, this muscle is found on both sides of the back and covers the middle layer muscles.

Basic Function of the Spine

Let's look at each of these layers in more detail. We'll consider how each layer is related to proper spine function and how they respond to low back pain.

The Deep Layer

With every movement of our body our spine moves at the roughly twenty-five spinal joints found throughout the spinal column. As mentioned in chapter one, the large bending movements of the spinal column are the result of smaller sliding and tilting motions occurring at individual spinal joints.

It is easy to appreciate the large bending movements of our spinal column which occur when we are getting in or out of a car, plugging in the vacuum cleaner or dancing the 'limbo' at the office New Year's party. Less obvious is the fact that some amount of spinal joint motion occurs when we walk, work at our computer or even raise our arm above our head. The sliding motions of the spinal joints are normally so small that even an x-ray will fail to capture them (although they have been measured in research laboratories using specialized equipment). The tilting motions however, are often large enough to be seen on x-rays.

The function of the deep layer is twofold. First, the discs and ligaments bind vertebrae together and to some extent, prevent the vertebrae from moving too far in any direction (the dog and leash analogy). If the sliding and tilting motions are not kept within certain limits, the disc or ligaments will be injured, and effective, comfortable spinal movement would not be possible. We'll keep in mind however, that even healthy discs and ligaments provide only a fraction of the stabilization required by our spinal column.

Second, the discs, small muscles and ligaments of the deep layer have the ability to 'sense' changes in the position of the many joints of the spinal column. They send this positional information directly to the nervous system. We are just now beginning to understand the significance of this position-sensing function of the deep layer. Indeed, it appears that our nervous system is extremely dependent on this position sense information when attempting to activate the various muscles which make our spine work.

Spinal Injury and the Deep Layer

If any part of the deep layer is injured, two serious problems develop. The injured joint will move excessively and the positional information normally sent to the nervous system from the joint will become impaired. Excess motion at spinal joints causes pain, pain which might be felt in the lower back or even into the leg. The lack of correct positional information, as well as the pain, makes it difficult for the nervous system to activate certain spinal muscles, primarily the middle layer muscles. This same series of events occurs in virtually all people with low back pain and can lead to even further problems as our spinal joints, discs and nerves are left unprotected.

More traditional exercise approaches for back injury rehabilitation and sports conditioning were based on a concept of spinal pathology that did not account for these critical problems. Establishing better control or activation of the middle layer muscles and developing an improved 'position sense' through the spine must be the main objectives of any low back rehabilitation program. As we will see in later sections, exercises designed to improve our position sense vary from easy to extremely difficult. This range of exercise challenge ensures that everyone can benefit from this aspect of the program.

The Middle Layer - Stabilizing the Spinal Column

Given the relative weakness of the spinal disc and ligaments, the job of stabilizing the spinal column is left to the muscles of the middle layer. Until recently, we failed to appreciate the importance of the middle layer muscles in this activity. Instead, we had assumed that the discs and ligaments alone prevented excessive motion at individual spinal joints.

We now know that the discs and ligaments provide only a small degree of stability and only at the extreme end range of a movement. It is the middle layer muscles which are responsible for the majority of the stabilization required to keep our back functioning properly and without pain.

Our trunk, or core, is the foundation of our entire body. The trunk acts like a platform from which our legs and arms function. If this platform is unstable, the muscles of the arms and legs will have to work harder to accomplish a given task. The shoulder and hip joints might also be exposed to unusually high stresses. To prevent these problems, a child's nervous system learns to pre-activate the middle layer muscles before any movements of the body. This has the effect of stabilizing individual spinal joints and then bracing the overall spinal column.

Once the spine is stable, movement in our limbs can occur efficiently, without disturbing our overall sense of balance or placing our various joints at risk. The degree to which the middle layer muscles are activated depends on the type and the intensity of the movement. Larger, more forceful movements will require greater amounts of stabilization of the spine in order to minimize motion of the vertebrae.

The trunk must be stable to allow our limbs to work at optimal efficiency. If our spine is not well stabilized, some part of the body will eventually become injured. The transversus abdominis, multifidus and quadratus lumborum are the key stabilizing muscles of the spine. The psoas muscle may well play an important role in stability also. Proper function and control of these middle layer muscles is of the utmost importance both in therapeutic stabilization for people with back pain and in stabilization-based conditioning programs for athletes.

Spine Injury and the Middle Layer

Researchers in the USA, Australia and Japan have shown that when the spine's deep layer is injured, the multifidus, a key stabilizing muscle which would normally protect the injured spinal joint, quickly shrinks by 25% and fails to activate correctly. This has been shown to occur as rapidly as 24 hours following spinal injury and to last indefinitely, even after a person's back pain appears to have settled. The loss of multifidus size occurs only at the injured joint, and only on the side which is injured.

Likewise, the transversus abdominis also fails to work correctly following back injury, often activating or contracting later than it should to adequately protect the spinal joints. These types of problems with stabilizing muscle are not a simple form of weakness, but a form of nervous system error. They occur because the nervous system is unable to activate the muscle at the correct time and to the appropriate degree.

This means that just when the spine needs extra support, the muscles which would normally supply that help become 'sluggish'. This makes exercises designed to specifically rehabilitate these stabilizing muscles even more critical to a successful rehabilitation program.

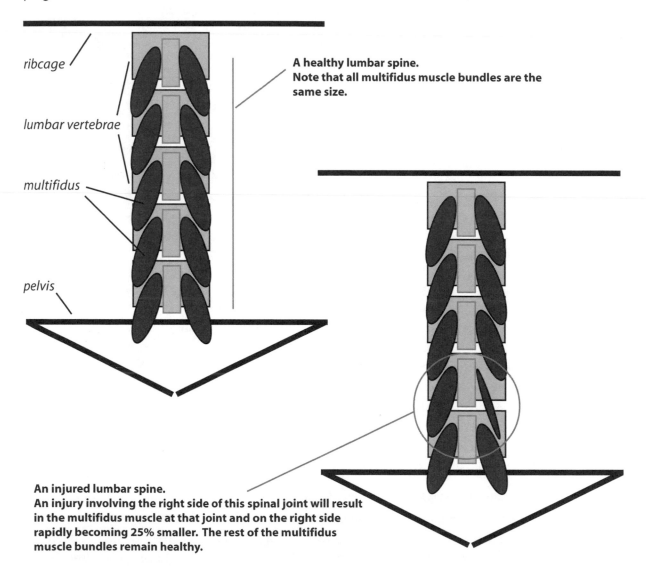

ribcage

A healthy lumbar spine.
Note that all multifidus muscle bundles are the same size.

lumbar vertebrae

multifidus

pelvis

An injured lumbar spine.
An injury involving the right side of this spinal joint will result in the multifidus muscle at that joint and on the right side rapidly becoming 25% smaller. The rest of the multifidus muscle bundles remain healthy.

The Outer Layer - Moving & Positioning the Spinal Column

Once individual spinal joints have been stabilized by the middle layer muscles, the larger muscles of the outer layer are used to position the spinal column as needed for lifting, bending and twisting. The long reach of these muscles, as well as their impressive thickness and mass, provides the ideal mechanism for spinal column movement and power generation.

Traditional back strengthening exercises designed to rehabilitate or prevent back injury worked the outer layer muscles as opposed to the middle layer muscles. In fact, if you look at some of the 'outer layer' exercises in chapters seven and eight, you'll find many exercises, now considered conditioning exercises, which were once used as rehabilitative exercises. This focus on the outer layer is the reason that traditional back exercise programs failed. Rehabilitation professionals strengthened the muscles which moved the spine, but neglected to rehabilitate those muscles which stabilize and protect it.

While the large outer layer muscles are certainly important, it is the middle layer muscles which suffer the neurologic control problems that follow any form of spinal injury or disease. For this reason, rehabilitation efforts must correct this problem of the middle layer prior to any strengthening of the outer layer. This, in essence, is the primary feature of the Australian spinal stabilization approach described in chapter five.

Spine Injury and the Outer Layer

When a spinal problem develops, whether due to an acute injury or a progressive wear and tear process, the nervous system has difficulty activating the protective middle layer muscles such as transversus and multifidus. While knowledge of this feature of spinal pain is relatively new, we have recognized for years that certain outer layer muscles tend to go into 'spasm' following more severe, acute injuries.

In the past, this spasm was interpreted as a primary problem related to the injury and therefore various efforts were made to treat it. Heat, stretching, massage, and muscle relaxant medications were prescribed to reduce muscle spasm, based on the idea that the spasm was the *cause* of the person's pain. Today we recognize that while spasm might be uncomfortable, it is merely a symptom of a greater underlying problem.

As the nervous system experiences difficulty activating the middle layer muscles following injury, it also recognizes that the injured spinal joint is in need of support. The spasm seen in an outer layer muscle is simply the nervous system's attempt to prevent movement at the vulnerable joint. Muscles such as the erector spinae have been known for some time to develop spasm near the site of injury. We are now recognizing that other muscles of the pelvis and hip regions suffer similar problems as the nervous system searches for alternative muscle mechanisms with which to support an unstable spinal joint.

Outer layer muscles, however, are not built for single joint stabilization. Therefore the nervous system must dramatically increase the level of activation or contraction in these big muscles to develop some degree of 'splinting' or immobilization at the injury site. The person with a back injury and outer layer muscle spasm will feel pain generated by the injured spinal column, along with an uncomfortable tightness due to the spasm. They feel as if they constantly need to stretch these 'tight' muscles. As we will see in coming chapters, older approaches to treating spinal injury emphasized the outer layer muscles via stretching, strengthening or massaging. Given our new understanding of spinal injury, it is easy to appreciate why these approaches failed so frequently.

Key Points So Far ...

1. ### Our Spinal Column Moves at Individual Spinal Joints
    ☞ the many joints of the spine move constantly in sliding and tilting directions with all movements of our body

    ☞ these motions must be controlled in order for the spinal column to move efficiently and safely

2. ### Stabilization of the Spinal Joints is Necessary for a Healthy Spine
    ☞ our very mobile spinal column is inherently unstable - the discs and ligaments once thought to be capable of handling the various stresses associated with everyday movements are relatively weak and fragile

    ☞ research has demonstrated that the spinal discs and ligaments will fail, or become injured, under only nine kg of mechanical stress while normal movements place stresses of 600 to 1700 kg through our spinal column

3. ### Spinal Muscle is Critical in Spinal Joint Stabilization
    ☞ if the spinal joints alone cannot tolerate the physical stress associated with everyday movement, then spinal muscles must provide the bulk of the stabilization needed for a healthy spine

4. ### The Nervous System is Critical in Spinal Joint Stabilization
    ☞ given that muscle is required to protect and stabilize spinal joints, the nervous system is also essential as muscle actions must be coordinated by the nervous system

    ☞ positional information from discs and ligaments provides a quick means of activating middle layer muscles built specifically to stabilize spinal joints

5.   Our Trunk is Made up of Three Layers, Each with a Specific Function

☞   the deep layer consists primarily of the vertebrae, the spinal discs and ligaments

☞   the function of the deep layer is to provide position sense information to the nervous system regarding the position of the joints of the spine

☞   the ligaments and discs of the deep layer also provide the spinal joints with a small degree of stability

☞   the middle layer of the trunk consists of medium size muscles responsible for stabilizing and protecting the joints of the spine in all postures

☞   the outer layer is made up of large, powerful muscles which can move the spine and maintain the overall posture of the spinal column, even against huge loads

6.   All Spinal Pathology Leads to Three Inter-Related Problems

☞   with either acute injury of the spinal joint structures, or the progressive wear and tear problems of the 'no-longer-twenty-years-old' spinal column, increased motion will develop at a spinal joint

☞   at the same time, protective stabilizing muscles of the trunk's middle layer will fail to work correctly as the nervous system develops an inability to optimally control these muscles

☞   outer layer muscles are then substituted for the middle layer muscles as the nervous system attempts to provide some degree of splinting at the injured joint - this is commonly known as muscle spasm

Chapter 3
The Unstable Spine

Low back injuries, by tradition, have most often been described as muscular injuries - injury and pain related to strained or 'pulled' muscles. This tendency to explain back injury as a muscular problem is largely due to older ideas about spinal column stability. Before it was recognized that our spinal column joints were quite fragile, the fact that the vast majority of people with low back pain had normal spinal x-rays was considered as proof that the spinal column and its joints were undamaged. It seemed logical therefore, to pin the blame for the person's back pain on some degree of muscle injury.

However, a thorough assessment of the person with back pain rarely produces the evidence or examination findings typical of a muscle injury. In the majority of cases, the person simply hadn't sustained the degree of physical trauma necessary to actually cause any tearing of muscle fibers (it takes a tremendous amount of stress to actually injure muscle in this way, especially the thick strong low back muscles). Furthermore, during physical examination of the back muscles it is rare to see positive tests indicating true muscle damage. If the examination of a person with low back pain routinely fails to turn up good evidence of muscle damage, why has the diagnosis of 'muscle strain' persisted for so long?

The traditional idea of spinal stability - that the spinal disc and ligaments were strong enough to support the spine by themselves - led to the belief that if a spinal x-ray showed no unusual or significant shifting at a spinal joint, the ligaments and discs must be healthy. The injured tissue must therefore be a muscle. However, research regarding the details of spinal joint motion has led to a very different conclusion.

Using specialized testing equipment, spinal researchers measured the amount of sliding and tilting at healthy spinal joints. Next, they stressed the joint until an injury occurred and then re-measured the joint motion. With stresses of only 6 - 7 kg, the joint would be injured. In some cases the disc would be injured, in others a ligament. Regardless of the type of injury, the amount of sliding movement at the injured joint would consistently increase by 400 to 600%, yet no significant change could be observed with an x-ray. In other words, x-rays are not sensitive enough to pick up the vast majority of spinal joint injuries.

If muscle strains are not the cause of back pain, then what is happening? There are likely four different pathways to spinal pathology and low back pain. We'll look at the actual diagnoses related to low back pain in the next chapter. For now, we'll simply consider the four most common mechanisms by which the spine becomes unstable.

Trauma

A sudden, high-force injury remains a very plausible cause of low back injury and pain. Falling down the stairs, a high-speed automobile accident, a particularly nasty body-check in a hockey game where a player's back is slammed into the boards - these injuries represent the degree of force involved with actual spine trauma. In such cases it is easy to appreciate how and why the spine was injured. With this degree of impact, the spine is at risk for the full spectrum of spinal injury from fractures of the vertebrae to relatively mild injuries of the spinal disc or ligaments or simple bruising of the soft tissues of the trunk.

While trauma is a very reasonable potential cause of low back pain, it remains a relatively rare event. Most people with low back pain have not experienced a truly traumatic event such as those described. Much more common is the situation where a person develops back pain without having done anything unusual or especially strenuous.

The No-Longer-Twenty-Years-Old Spine

Those of us who are no longer twenty years old may not be pleased to hear this, but as our spine becomes older, it goes through certain changes related to its age. Through a process of simple wear and tear, key parts of the spinal joints begin to wear out a little. The disc becomes thinner and more brittle, even cracked in places. As this happens, the disc can't perform either its minor role as a stabilizer of the spinal joint or its key role as a position sensor (see chapter 1) to the extent that it did when it was younger and healthier. Both of these problems will lead to instability at a spinal joint. Once an instability has developed, the person is at greater risk of pain and even further injury.

'Genetic' Problems of the Spine

Another cause of low back pain is a group of disorders in which a person's spine develops in an unusual way. These include scoliosis, a problem of the spine which most frequently affects adolescent girls. A scoliosis is an abnormal curve of the spine, usually in a side-to-side fashion. Many of these are quite mild and may never lead to symptoms. Indeed, they might not even be noticed except by a health care professional. A more severe scoliosis may cause such an extreme amount of curvature that the patient has difficulty breathing.

In these cases she may need to have surgery to correct the problem. Other examples of such disorders include spinal stenosis, a condition affecting older people in which the spinal canal, which encloses the spinal cord, becomes progressively more narrow. Eventually, there is not enough space for the spinal cord and it becomes compressed during certain types of movement. Both scoliosis and spinal stenosis can become quite severe and debilitating.

Another problem which is likely genetic in origin involves the 'loose' or hypermobile spine which lends itself so well to elite performance in ballet or gymnastics. People with this sort of spine have excessive motion at their spinal joints and are sometimes referred to as being 'double jointed' at other joints as well. The person whose spine is naturally hypermobile likely has a higher risk of back problems simply because it is so much harder for their nervous system and muscles to control or stabilize their excess joint motion.

The Software Crash Theory of Back Injury

The following scenario is fairly familiar to most people. After standing and chatting with a friend for a few minutes, you've shifted most of your weight to one foot. For no apparent reason, your supporting knee suddenly buckles a little; not enough that you fall, but you notice it nonetheless. What just happened?

Once researchers recognized the importance of muscle in stabilizing our spine, it was immediately apparent that the nervous system must also play a significant role in stabilizing and protecting our spinal joints. The process of controlling the 632 muscles in our body so that the 280 joints in our body are at all times stable and protected is an enormously complex task. To make matters more complex, each of our 632 muscles is actually composed of hundreds or thousands of individual muscle fiber bundles; each of these has its own nerve and functional ability. In reality then, we likely have about 300,000 'muscles' which our nervous system can activate in virtually any combination, depending on the movement dynamics of the moment.

A growing number of researchers and clinicians now consider it likely that nervous system error is an important and frequent cause of low back injury. In the case of the knee that buckles, the nervous system makes a mistake; the brain 'forgets' to keep the large muscle at the front of the thigh activated, and the knee suddenly gives out. In the lower back, if even one of the three or four key stabilizing muscles is not activated correctly, a spinal joint may be exposed to injury.

What evidence do we have that this sort of nervous system 'glitch' can cause low back injury? Certainly, much is circumstantial at this point. However, there is one scientific study which captured such an event in the lab. We'll look at the circumstantial evidence first then describe the research supporting this potential cause of back injury.

Given the absolute need for muscular control of spinal joint motion, the nervous system must be involved in maintaining this stability as muscles only do what the nervous system instructs them to do. We'll also remember that the lumbar spine can withstand only nine kilograms of stress before its discs or ligaments sustain injury.

Let's first consider the large number of people who sustain sudden and sometimes severe back injury without any trauma. The person might have been doing something very ordinary such as walking or rolling out of bed in the morning, yet they sustained a significant injury and felt a large amount of pain. Examples from my practice over the past couple of years include a dance teacher who walked across her studio and experienced sudden and excruciating pain in her back and leg. On examination a few days later, it was found that she had a herniated lumbar disc. Another person reached across his dining room table for a salt shaker and had a sudden and flash-like pain near his middle back. In his case, a small joint between a rib and a vertebrae had moved abnormally resulting in his symptoms. My next door neighbor, after years of increasingly frequent low back pain episodes, went to get out of bed one morning and suddenly experienced the most severe back and leg pain he had ever known. An MRI identified a massive disc herniation which would require surgery to correct.

People with similar back pain stories are all too common. Health care professionals have, for the longest time, explained such sudden injury by saying to these people "well, it must have been the straw that broke the camel's back". We had no more reasonable answer at that time for why such low risk, everyday activities could lead to such big problems.

Once we recognized the importance of continuous and essentially perfect neurologic control of multiple low back muscles, it became apparent that the nervous system simply couldn't perform such an enormous task without the occasional glitch. Like those complicated computer operating systems that crash for no apparent reason, perhaps the human operating system, the central nervous system, is prone to similar glitches.

Dr. Stuart McGill, a respected spine researcher from the University of Waterloo in Canada, was conducting an experiment examining the motion of the spine during heavy lifting. With competitive weightlifters performing their normal lifts in his lab, Dr. McGill monitored the motion of their spines using x-ray technology which allowed for the spine to be seen in real-time, full motion video. One weightlifter sustained an injury during the experiment and was unable to continue.

When Dr. McGill reviewed the video x-ray, he noticed something quite unusual. Although the weightlifter had maintained a consistent *overall* curve through his lower back from one repetition to the next, somehow his nervous system failed to maintain correct control at a single joint in the lumbar spine. For no apparent reason, his nervous system failed to adequately activate his middle layer muscles, and a single spinal joint was allowed to over-rotate by 0.5 degrees. The nervous system failed to activate the required muscle at the right time, and either a disc or a ligament was damaged, allowing the joint to move too far (he damaged his vertebral 'dog leash').

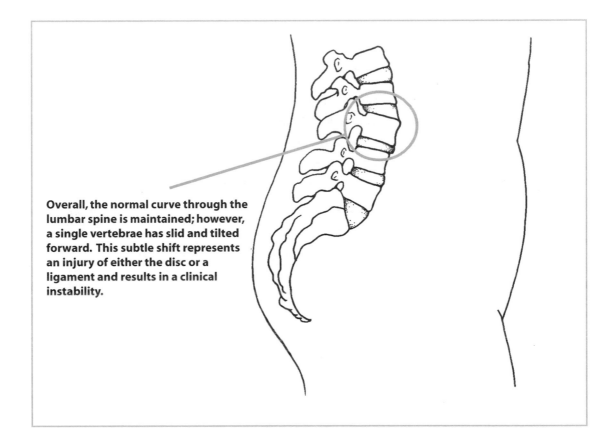

Overall, the normal curve through the lumbar spine is maintained; however, a single vertebrae has slid and tilted forward. This subtle shift represents an injury of either the disc or a ligament and results in a clinical instability.

Interestingly, the fact that his lumbar curve was maintained meant that his outer layer muscles had continued to work correctly. The middle layer muscles responsible for controlling the small motions at individual spinal joints simply failed to activate when they were needed. The nervous system sustained a small 'crash', and a joint was unsupported at a vulnerable moment. The spinal disc and/or ligaments at that joint were stressed beyond their tolerance of nine kilograms, leading to the weightlifter's injury.

While there is admittedly little direct scientific evidence of these events, there is now at least a more reasonable, research-based explanation for those people whose back was injured while they performed a relatively normal activity. There is, in fact, a great deal more evidence for this explanation as to the cause of such injuries than there is for any other.

Instability: The Common Denominator

Regardless of whether your back pain began as a result of trauma, age-related changes or a 'software crash' of your nervous system, if a spinal disc, ligament or other spinal joint structure is injured or pathologic, your spine will have experienced two changes following your first episode of significant low back pain. First, there is an excess amount of motion at your problematic spinal joint. Second, the middle layer muscles which should be controlling this motion do not work correctly. This combination of problems is now referred to as a *clinical spinal instability*.

This might seem too bold and all-encompassing a statement - that regardless of the actual cause, all low back pain leads to instability. There are those that argue that discs and ligaments heal in about six to eight weeks and that beyond that point in time the pain should be gone. To some extent, these statements are correct. At the same time, it is incorrect to say that once the injury has 'healed', the problem is resolved.

In cases where there has been an injury of a disc or ligament, these structures will indeed heal. The excess motion persists because the healing - being less than perfect - fails to return the disc or ligament to its original mechanical ability. In cases where age related changes are the cause of back pain, there is no 'healing' to occur. The wear and tear process only worsens with time.

The other aspect of instability involves the neurologic error that develops along with low back pain. A lack of proper neurologic drive to middle layer muscles such as the multifidus and the transversus abdominis has been shown to persist indefinitely in people with both traumatic injury and wear and tear-type back problems. Once developed, this does not resolve even though the person's symptoms might improve substantially, and in a relatively short time. This loss of normal nervous system control of transversus and multifidus is quite a different problem from that of simple muscular weakness.

The multifidus muscle is actually several distinct bundles of muscle. In the healthy low back, all multifidus bundles are essentially the same size. Within twenty-four hours of a sudden low back injury affecting a single spinal joint, the multifidus muscle adjacent to the injured joint will shrink by twenty-five percent (see page 18). That the loss of multifidus size occurs so rapidly and that this loss occurs only at the spinal joint which is injured, is proof that this is not a form of traditional muscular weakness. Muscles that become weak in the normal sense take weeks to get smaller and the loss of size is always similar throughout the entire muscle.

Other research has shown that when a spinal ligament is injured, the multifidus muscle adjacent to the injured structure stops contracting as it did prior to the injury. Similarly, the activation of the transversus abdominis muscle is delayed when people have any form of spinal pathology. Changes of this type can only occur due to a loss of normal neurologic control over these muscles.

The Evolution of Back Pain

Ninety percent of people with sudden low back pain will have their pain resolve substantially or even fully, with or without treatment of any kind, within six to eight weeks. This is a tremendously important fact for both health care professionals and patients to keep in mind. This all but proves that whatever we in the medical and rehabilitation professions have been doing over the past fifty years to treat acute low back pain, it has often been no more effective than the patient caring for themselves. This is a sobering statistic to be sure.

However, this fact should be kept in context. Of the vast majority of people whose pain settles within eight weeks, up to seventy percent will go on to experience recurrent low back pain. They are not 'healed' simply because their initial pain went away; they will often continue to have brief episodes of low back pain every few months, while otherwise feeling more or less fine.

The research at this time conclusively demonstrates that any form of spinal pathology involving the disc, ligaments or other joint structures will lead to what is now known as a clinical spinal instability. The research also proves that an instability of this type will leave the spine vulnerable and the person at higher risk for future episodes of back pain.

The Evolution of Back Pain Therapy

Fortunately, this same research has led to a form of rehabilitative or therapeutic exercise designed specifically to address these problems. Clinical studies have shown that patients who were treated with the Australian spinal stabilization approach are up to twelve times less likely to experience repeat episodes of low back pain as compared to people treated with more traditional approaches. Chapter five will discuss this approach in detail.

Now that we have some sense of how the spine can become injured or pathologic and why people with back pain are so at risk for future episodes of low back pain, let's look at some of the actual diagnostic terms used to define the various types of spinal problems.

Chapter 4
Understanding Your Back Pain

Most people are unfamiliar with the medical terms used to describe different types and causes of low back pain. This chapter will outline the various medical diagnostic terms used to identify the more common forms of low back pain. The degree to which we can reasonably expect therapeutic spinal stabilization to be effective with each type of problem is also discussed.

The Herniated Disc

In the case of a true disc herniation, the disc between two vertebrae develops a bulge, putting pressure on the large nerve passing just behind the disc. Back problems caused by a herniated spinal disc are relatively rare. In fact only about three to five percent of people with low back pain have this problem. When it does occur, the disc puts pressure on a nerve resulting in back and leg pain. Usually, the person with a disc herniation will have leg pain which is worse than their back pain, as well as numbness and muscle weakness somewhere in the lower leg or foot. This condition will almost always lead to changes in the normal muscle reflexes at the knee or ankle as well.

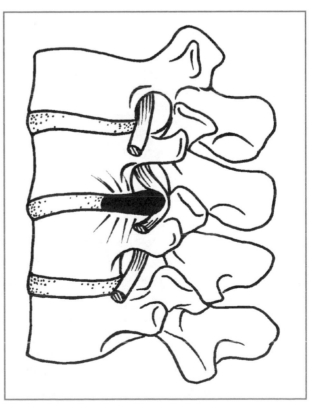

The lumbar spine shown from the left demonstrating a herniated disc between the third and fourth lumbar vertebrae

Unfortunately, many people with less severe back problems are told they have a 'slipped disc' or 'sciatica'. For the record, spinal discs do not 'slip' out of place and sciatica is a vague term which only describes back pain which spreads down the leg. Spreading leg pain may or may not be due to an injured spinal disc, and therefore is not, by itself, a conclusive indication of disc herniation-related back pain.

Stabilization Training and Disc Herniation

This is one of the more serious types of back injury treated by physical therapists, as it has the potential to require corrective surgery whereas most other back problems do not. However, more surgeons today seem willing to try non-surgical approaches (i.e., physical therapy) before suggesting an operation. Whether a person's early management involves surgery or not, the main goal of treatment in the early stages is to alleviate the compression on the nerve root. In many instances, this can be accomplished non-surgically. However, if the degree of disc injury is too extensive (in the case, for instance, of a massive herniation of the disc), surgery will likely be necessary.

While therapeutic spinal stabilization exercises (see chapter five) may be initiated early in this situation (so long as a pain-free exercise position may be found) the primary goal in the early or acute stage must be to alleviate compression of the spinal nerve. Stabilization exercises should not be progressed in earnest until compression of the spinal nerve has been completely relieved. Once the nerve compression is resolved, either by surgery or physical therapy techniques, therapeutic stabilization exercises should be used to improve the nervous system's ability to control the muscles which provide the primary support and protection of the spine and its injured disc.

There are now numerous studies showing that disc herniation injury consistently results in a significant series of changes involving the multifidus muscle. The multifidus adjacent to the injured disc quickly shrinks due to diminished activation from the nervous system. This has been shown to happen as early as 24 hours following injury. Even when surgical correction of a person's disc herniation is successful, their multifidus remains small and under-activated for at least five years following the surgery. Traditional low back rehabilitation programs (i.e., programs based in some way on muscle strengthening) do not correct this deficit nor improve the function of this muscle.

Therapeutic spinal stabilization exercises which target the middle layer muscles are more likely to offset these problems and ensure an optimal recovery from injury. Australian researchers have demonstrated that spinal stabilization exercises will re-train the multifidus and restore it to its pre-injury level of function much more quickly and completely than traditional methods. No other rehabilitation approach has been shown to accomplish this critical objective.

Mechanical Low Back Pain

Mechanical low back pain has become a catch-all phrase for a number of different problems affecting the many joints, discs, ligaments and muscles of the spine. Many health care professionals prefer to use terms which more specifically describe the actual injury sustained by the patient. This is determined through a comprehensive examination of the patient in which the various joints, muscles and nerves of the spine are tested in a systematic fashion, leading to a diagnosis of the problem. The following are more specific diagnostic terms describing the various 'mechanical' problems people can experience.

Sprain

The term sprain describes an injury to a spinal ligament due to some form of trauma - a fall, twist or other accident. In chapter three we discussed how the 'software crash' theory of spinal injury may also lead to an injured or sprained ligament. Since ligaments help stabilize the small sliding and tilting motions of the spinal joints, an injured ligament will allow a joint to move excessively, resulting in pain.

Strain

Similar to a ligament sprain, a strain always occurs due to trauma, but in this case, the injury involves a muscle. Healthy muscles do not tear unless subjected to a significant force thus it is not possible to wake up in the morning with a true muscle strain, a torn muscle, if the person did not experience some kind of accident. The person with a muscle strain injury will have sustained some kind of traumatic event and felt pain immediately. Sprains and strains will vary in severity based on the extent to which the ligament or muscle fibers are torn. As mentioned in chapter two however, strain injuries of the lower back muscles are rare.

Subluxation

This refers to a joint injury where a spinal joint becomes 'stuck' and unable to move fully through its sliding and tilting motions. Subluxation may occur with or without trauma. The injury sustained by Dr. McGill's weightlifter (see page 25) is an example of both a ligament sprain and a subluxation injury.

The weightlifter's middle layer muscles failed to activate correctly leading to excessive stress on a spinal ligament. When the ligament failed, or sprained, the spinal joint moved an excess 0.5 degrees resulting in a subluxation. This is not enough excess movement to be easily noticed on a normal spinal x-ray but it clearly demonstrates that a very small amount of incorrect spinal motion can lead to significant injury and pain. Subluxations may occur at any level of the spine.

Hypermobility

This term also refers to a joint problem. Unlike subluxations in which the joint becomes 'stuck', the hypermobile joint develops too much motion. Usually the hypermobile spinal joint has lost the normal degree of stabilization provided by its disc or ligaments. This leads to abnormally large amounts of sliding and tilting at the joint. Hypermobilities may be due to injury, certain forms of athletic training (e.g., gymnastics) or the fact that some people are just born with 'loose joints'. A hypermobile joint may remain relatively painless if the stabilizing muscles surrounding the joint are able to control its excess motion.

Osteoarthritis (OA)

Osteoarthritis (OA) is a wear and tear problem involving the protective layer of cartilage which lines our joints. Everyone will have developed some degree of osteoarthritis by the age of sixty, because our joints wear out somewhat over time. As cartilage does not contain pain nerves, healthy joint cartilage can tolerate significant compression forces without the joint becoming painful. Unfortunately, this protective layer wears thin over time leaving the bone underneath the cartilage exposed to the forces which occur normally with all movements. Since bones do have pain nerves, these forces can lead to significant amounts of pain.

Osteoarthritic changes are quite common in the joints of the lower back and neck. From a stabilization perspective, the pain and swelling that develops at the arthritic joint leads to the 'faulty cylinder syndrome' described earlier (page 11 & 12). The nervous system has difficulty activating muscles such as transversus and multifidus and this leads to more problems at the painful joint. Stabilization and gentle stretching exercises are the best exercise prescription for people with OA-related problems. A physical therapist is an excellent resource in choosing the safest, most effective exercises to control this type of back pain.

Stabilization Training and Mechanical Back Pain

Sprains, strains, subluxations, hypermobilities and osteoarthritic problems may require other forms of treatment in the acute stage to safely and effectively treat and resolve the problem. This depends on the severity of the injury or condition. A health care professional can discuss the most suitable options for each person's injury. Therapeutic stabilization exercises should become the focus of treatment as soon as possible. In most cases, these exercises can begin immediately. Performed correctly, therapeutic stabilization exercises will not increase your symptoms. Each person with mechanical low back pain, regardless of their diagnosis, will need to improve the function of their middle layer muscles before they can consider their risk of re-injury to be reduced.

Degenerative Disc Disease

As people get older, spinal discs lose some of their elasticity and water content - they actually 'dry out' to some extent. They become thinner, more brittle and even develop little cracks along their edges. While there is some disagreement as to where the pain of degenerative disc disease actually comes from, a thinner, dryer, more brittle disc is no longer as good a stabilizer as it was when it was healthier. Thus with this condition, some degree of spinal instability will develop.

Stabilization Training and Degenerative Disc Disease

As with spinal osteoarthritis, degenerative disc disease cannot be 'cured' by either medical or rehabilitative means. However, the pain associated with these conditions can be reduced, sometimes quite significantly, by re-training the middle layer muscles to do their proper job. If these stabilizing muscles can be made more effective, the abnormal motions of the small spinal joints can be brought under control, resulting in decreased pain.

Spondylolisthesis (spaun-di-lo-lies-thee-sis)

The vertebrae of the spine can be thought of as having a front and rear half. The front half consists of a large block of bone called the body. The rear half is made up of the 'tube' which surrounds the spinal cord along with three odd-looking projections to which muscles and ligaments attach. In a very small number of people, the portion of the vertebrae where the front and back halves meet develops incorrectly. In these unusual vertebrae, the region where the front and back halves attach is actually formed of a thick, heavy connective tissue instead of bone. Sometimes these areas of connective tissue detach, allowing the front half of the vertebrae to separate slightly from the back half.

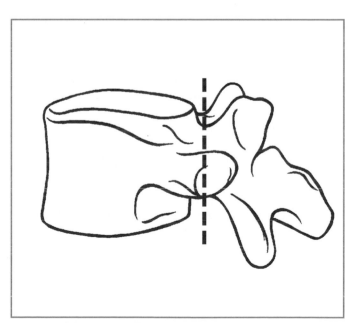

In spondylolithesis the front half of the vertebrae detaches slightly from the rear half along this line

Stabilization Training and Spondylolisthesis

For people with this condition, spinal stabilization exercises can provide some of the best pain control available. As with degenerative disc disease and OA, spondylolisthesis provides a great challenge to the 'position sensors' of the spine. Thus, while therapeutic stabilization exercises can be effective, they must be performed regularly in order to be helpful in this situation.

Spinal Stenosis

If we were to look down the length of the spinal column from above, we would see that the shape of the individual vertebrae allows for the spinal column to have a hollow center, like a paper towel tube. In reality, the hollow center is where the spinal cord is found. Therefore the spinal cord, carrying all the messages between our brain and body, is located inside a 'tube' of bone formed by the vertebrae.

In a small percentage of older people, this tube begins to get more narrow as new, abnormal bone growth occurs inside the spinal canal where the spinal cord is located. This can lead to a variety of problems from pain to numbness to muscular weakness involving the lower half of the body as the spinal cord becomes compressed within the tighter canal.

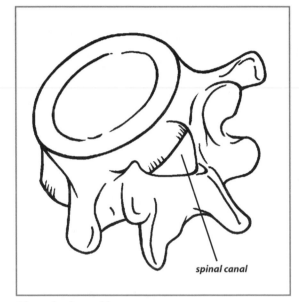

spinal canal

The spinal canal becomes more narrow in spinal stenosis

Stabilization Training and Spinal Stenosis

Unfortunately, there is very little that can be done to correct the actual problem of spinal stenosis from an exercise perspective. The narrowing of the spinal canal will not be affected by any form of exercise nor any form of medical treatment presently available. A surgery whereby part of the vertebrae is removed - a *laminectomy* - might be performed to lessen the pressure on the spinal cord. If this is done, some of the middle layer muscles at that joint will also be removed. Therefore, in people who have had this surgery, therapeutic stabilization may be helpful in minimizing the post-surgical instability which can be expected to develop.

If the person with spinal stenosis happens to have some other spinal problem in addition to their stenosis (e.g., OA or degenerative disc disease) they may notice some improvement in their symptoms with better functioning middle layer muscles depending on how much of their pain was related to the stenosis versus the other condition.

This is a complicated medical condition and thus any rehabilitative exercise program should be designed by a licensed health care professional familiar with therapeutic stabilization exercise.

Rheumatoid Arthritis (RA)

Rheumatoid or Inflammatory Arthritis is a serious medical problem which can affect almost any system of the body. The joints, lungs, kidneys, eyes and hearts of people with RA may develop various problems related to this disease. While not completely understood, RA is currently thought to be a form of autoimmune disease. This means the body apparently fails to recognize its own tissues and initiates something of a self-destructive process. Because of the wide range of possible complications, this condition should be managed by a medical specialist trained specifically in RA-related conditions.

From the joint perspective, the disease process can effect virtually any joint in the body. RA damages and eventually destroys the tissues found within the joints, namely the protective cartilage and some of the ligaments. This type of damage leaves the joint very unstable, and therefore quite vulnerable and in need of protection. For this and other reasons it is important that people who have been diagnosed with RA are treated by a medical specialist, a rheumatologist, and if necessary, a physical therapist skilled in the treatment of this condition.

Stabilization Training and Rheumatoid Arthritis

An interesting feature of RA is the fact that it almost never causes low back pain. Dr. Evelyn Sutton, a Halifax rheumatologist, stated: "while I try never to say never with regard to anything medical, rheumatoid arthritis should never be blamed as the cause of someone's back pain. This isn't to say that a person with RA can't have low back pain, it simply means their low back pain will be caused by something other than RA." Thus, the person who has RA and low back pain needs to be examined by a health care professional to determine the reason for their sore back.

While stabilization therapy will often prove helpful for people with RA, each and every person with RA will experience a unique set of challenges related to their disease. For this reason it is best that the person with RA has a spinal stabilization program designed specifically for them. If you have been diagnosed with any form of rheumatoid arthritis, please consult with a licensed health care professional before beginning any exercise program.

Atypical Back Pain:
When Instability is Not a Cause of Low Back Pain

A very small number of people, probably less than one percent, will have back pain for reasons other than those described to this point. These people will have back pain which may be identical in *feeling* to the various types mentioned in this chapter, yet their spinal column and muscles work as they are supposed to. In such situations the pain is real, it can be extremely intense - even disabling - yet it does not have an instability-related cause as do the more common types of low back pain. To appreciate these unusual conditions we need to look more closely at the complex issue of 'pain' itself, rather than the anatomy and mechanical behavior of the spine.

Despite that fact that pain is currently a very 'hot' research topic, little is understood about the function of the nervous system with regard to pain. What we do know suggests that pain is tremendously more complicated than most of us have appreciated. As children, we learn to believe that if some part of our body hurts, then that part of the body must be the *source* of our pain. Certainly in many situations shoulder pain is indicative of a shoulder problem, ankle pain an ankle problem and low back pain, a spinal problem. Unfortunately, the nervous system has the potential to make our experience of physical pain much more complex and confusing than this.

The sensation of pain is transmitted, processed and experienced throughout various levels of our nervous system. Peripheral nerves, the spinal cord, the autonomic nervous system, the conscious and sub-conscious regions of our brain, our hormonal system - all have some ability to impact on our experience of pain. The fact that so many parts of the human nervous system participate in the pain experience makes it possible for our low back pain to be caused by something other than a spinal instability. These other causes include physical problems in other parts of the body, rare infections or tumors of the spine itself, even stress.

The internal organs of the body are connected to the central nervous system via the autonomic nervous system. These connections occur throughout the middle part of the spine (the thoracic spine). Some people who have hard-to-pinpoint, non-specific pain in the center of the thoracic spine may in fact have back pain which is due to some degree of pathology or dysfunction in an internal organ. Others may have hip joint problems which manifest as low back pain. Conversely, some people will develop rare infections or even tumors in the spinal column itself. None of these situations involve the mechanical features of spinal instability.

The potential for stress to in some way affect physical pain has been suspected for some time. However, only recently have scientists identified any neurological or physiological mechanisms by which this might occur. During the late 1990's, researchers discovered new nervous system pathways and previously unknown interactions between the peripheral nervous system and normal hormonal mechanisms relating to stress. These findings strongly support the suggestion that stress can affect both the intensity and duration of a pain experience, and may even *cause* physical pain in the absence of physical pathology.

Spinal Stabilization and Atypical Back Pain

It should be apparent to most people that pain, regardless of its origin, is a symptom of some other problem. Pain is the reason we seek treatment but we know that the cause of the pain must be found for treatment to be successful. Most people with low back pain will have a combined mechanical and neurological dysfunction involving a spinal joint leading to a clinical spinal instability. These people will do very well with treatment designed specifically for this problem - that is, therapeutic stabilization exercises.

Likewise, the person whose symptoms are due to one of the more atypical causes of low back pain will only see a resolution of their problem once it is properly identified and then treated accordingly. If a person has a spinal infection, they need treatment other than stabilization exercises. If a person's spine functions normally but they are under significant stress at home or at work, it may be that their back pain has more to do with a stress-related reaction than a clinical instability. Again, treatment specific to the cause must be sought.

Summary

Today, a growing number of researchers and health care professionals recognize that the majority of spinal pathologies result in a clinical instability. In this regard the research cannot be more clear. As such, the majority of people with low back pain will benefit from well designed therapeutic stabilization exercises. There is simply no other approach which addresses the key problems inherent to most forms of spinal pathology - excess spinal joint motion combined with middle layer muscle dysfunction - as directly as does the Australian approach.

The challenge with these exercises is the fact that as the joint becomes unstable the 'deep layer' of the spine has difficulty developing and sending accurate positional information to the nervous system. Without good quality positional information it becomes harder for the nervous system to activate the very stabilizing muscles required to solve the problem. For this reason especially, clinical instabilities can be very difficult to manage. A strong commitment on the part of the patient is required in order to control their problem. It is essential that people with spinal instability perform their stabilization exercises carefully and faithfully. Despite the person's best efforts however, in some extreme cases the instability is too severe to correct with exercise, and surgery may be required. While the surgery - a *spinal fusion* - will prevent the unstable joint from moving, the surgery will not correct the muscle dysfunction which will have developed both prior to and following the operation. In these situations, once the person has recovered sufficiently from their surgery, they should begin stabilization exercises under the guidance of a qualified health care professional.

Chapter 5
Therapeutic Spinal Stabilization

Many back pain 'treatment options' have been promoted over the years as different health care professionals, working with the best information available, tried to devise methods of providing good rehabilitative care for people with bad backs. Unfortunately, these 'treatment options' were developed at a time when the spine was thought to be a stable structure. As such these treatment options did not account for the instability of the spine, the absolute need for middle layer muscular support of spinal joints nor the back pain-related loss of nervous system control of the middle layer muscles.

The majority of these options were based on the assumption that the injured person's abdominal and back muscles were weak and that strengthening exercises would in some way be therapeutic. However, current research has proven that the person with low back pain doesn't have back pain because they have weak trunk muscles. People have ongoing back pain because their nervous system can no longer activate certain middle layer muscles properly.

As the research discussed in the previous chapters made its way into medical journals and textbooks, other research detailing the success rates of traditional spinal rehabilitation methods was also published. The news has not been very satisfying from the perspective of the health care profession. Ninety percent of people with acute low back pain will have their pain resolve within eight weeks, regardless of the type of traditional treatment they receive, regardless of whether they are treated at all. Worse still, seventy percent of those who fully recover in eight weeks can expect to experience progressive episodes of low back pain in the future.

The research regarding our success with back pain is definitive. Traditional approaches to the problems associated with spinal pathology have been woefully ineffective at treating acute episodes of back pain and in preventing future episodes of back pain.

"My back pain went away with yoga classes ..."

A person with back pain might well have relief of their pain while participating in yoga or pilates classes, attending physical therapy or chiropractic treatment, or by swimming laps in a pool. It is natural for this person to then associate the resolution of their pain with the 'therapeutic' activity they were involved in at the time their pain settled. Although there is a certain intuitive 'correct-ness' about this association, we recognize that while walking, stretching exercises or tai chi might help one person's back pain, the same activity may well make someone else's pain worse. For every person who feels better with yoga (or physical therapy or pilates or swimming) there are probably three people who didn't realize any benefit from the same activity, and even one or two whose pain worsened.

Although it is normal for people to make these intuitive associations between an activity and the 'fixing' of their back problem, health care professionals are expected to have an appreciation for the scientific literature and in this regard the research is clear. Acute back pain will clear up within eight weeks while attending physical therapy, chiropractic, yoga or pilates classes, even reflexology, in ninety percent of people. Acute low back pain will also clear up in ninety percent of people even if they do nothing about it! When a large number of people with back pain are considered, it turns out that not one of these 'treatment options' is significantly more effective at improving the pain associated with a low back problem than is waiting for the pain to resolve on its own.

An award-winning study published in 1999 in the medical journal *Spine* compared physiotherapy, low impact aerobics classes and back strengthening exercises for their ability to improve pain levels in people with chronic low back troubles. By the end of the study, there were no differences in pain relief between groups. Attending a low-impact fitness class led by a fitness instructor was just as effective at improving chronic back pain as was traditional physiotherapy provided by a university-educated physiotherapist. The fact that traditional rehabilitative treatment is no more effective than fitness classes (or doing nothing at all) is good evidence of the fact that our traditional treatments have not been able to correct the underlying problems associated with painful backs. Until very recently, these underlying problems were unknown to us.

Traditional physical therapy or chiropractic exercises, swimming, walking, low impact aerobics, yoga, tai chi and pilates in many ways seem like very different forms of exercise. Yet in two fundamental ways they are quite similar; they each have the potential to improve muscular performance and they all place extraordinary muscular control demands on the central nervous system (while we often take them for granted, even the simplest movements are very challenging from a nervous system/muscular control standpoint). In order to perform the movement component of such exercises, support the weight of the body and adequately stabilize the spinal joints, our nervous system and trunk muscles must be operating normally.

Unfortunately, as we've only recently discovered, the person with low back pain no longer has a 'normal' nervous system. People with low back pain are unable to adequately activate muscles such as transversus abdominis and multifidus in any movement situation, whether it is something as simple as sitting upright or as complex as a yoga posture. People with low back pain have a nervous system that continually compensates for its inability to properly activate middle layer muscles by excessively activating outer layer muscles in an attempt to protect the spine. If these compensations were effective even fifty percent of the time, we wouldn't see so many people experiencing ongoing episodes of low back pain.

Exercise forms like those mentioned previously have the potential to improve muscular performance by increasing either the strength or endurance of our muscles. However, to do this, the nervous system must be able to properly activate the muscle. In the case of the person with typical low back pain, such exercises overwhelm the nervous system's capacity to control the middle layer muscles, leading to increased activation of the outer layer muscles. Muscles that already work properly will only work harder while the dysfunctional muscles remain impaired. In effect, such exercises only serve to train our compensatory activation patterns. This is the primary reason our traditional approaches to low back pain rehabilitation have not been more successful.

Strengthening exercises of any kind are, in reality, not that unique from the bending, twisting, and reaching movements people perform throughout the day. The only difference is in regard to the intensity of the movement. If after several months or even years of going about the normal activities of everyday life (which many people with episodic low back pain routinely do) why is it that people with low back problems still have one isolated segment of their multifidus muscle which remains smaller than the rest of the muscle? Why haven't these daily activities resulted in an equal strengthening effect and thus an equal size throughout the multifidus muscle? The reason is the lack of proper nervous system activation of the specific portion of the muscle which is adjacent to the pathologic spinal joint. Without ideal nervous system control, normal everyday activities as well as traditional strengthening exercises will fail to correct the problem.

The Australian Spinal Stabilization Method

A study published in the journal *Spine* in 2001 evaluated the Australian approach to therapeutic spinal stabilization. The study demonstrated that patients with acute, first-episode low back pain corrected the nervous system error which caused their multifidus and transversus to work poorly, fully restoring the proper size of their multifidus muscle.

Most importantly, the patients who were treated with the Australian approach were *twelve times* less likely to experience repeat back pain during the first year following their treatment. Over a three year follow-up period, the only spinal stabilization patients who reported *any* back pain were those who had sustained an entirely new traumatic injury.

Regarding the treatment of low back pain, success rates such as these are unheard of in the scientific literature. No other method of back pain treatment has ever been shown to be so completely successful at correcting the persistent problems that develop once the spine becomes injured and in preventing future episodes of back pain. While these results are certainly unique, no other approach to spinal rehabilitation has been based upon such a comprehensive understanding of spinal dysfunction and low back pain.

The Australian research-physiotherapists who developed this approach based their work on several important features of the most recent research related to back pain. These were listed at the end of chapter two. The most critical of these are repeated here:

All Spinal Pathology Leads to Three Inter-Related Problems:

☞ with either acute injury of the spinal joint structures, or slowly progressive wear and tear problems of the 'no-longer-twenty-years-old' spinal column, increased motion will develop at a spinal joint

☞ at the same time, protective stabilizing muscles of the trunk's middle layer will fail to work correctly as the nervous system develops an inability to activate or control these muscles optimally

☞ outer layer muscles are then substituted for the middle layer muscles in an attempt by the nervous system to provide some degree of splinting at the injured joint - this is commonly known as muscle spasm

The approach developed by these physiotherapists was designed to specifically correct the key problems identified above. The exercises will likely seem unusual to most people because they are to be done gently, with minimal exertion. This is not to say that they are easy. In fact they are some of the most challenging therapeutic exercises ever designed. These exercises are, however, more effective than any other form of treatment in halting the cycle of episodic low back pain so common in people with bad backs.

People with any form of low back pain should do all they can to locate a health care professional who uses the Australian approach in their practice. This is the best option for two reasons. First, if you have any amount of low back pain it must be correctly diagnosed before beginning any form of therapy. Second, these exercises, while being the most scientific and research-proven available for people with low back pain, are very difficult to perform correctly.

Other authors have suggested that the re-training of these muscles is easy and can be done independently of a health care professional using relatively simple strengthening exercises. This is not an accurate representation of the research, nor the clinical reality of this approach. The Australian method of spinal stabilization is difficult to do without guidance from an experienced clinician; however, it will be worth the effort and time spent as it is so much more effective than other treatment approaches.

Stage One - Isolated Transversus Abdominis Activation

The key to this approach involves improving the nervous system's ability to activate muscles such as transversus and multifidus in a more appropriate fashion. This is accomplished by learning to voluntarily activate these muscles in near-perfect isolation. In fact, it is entirely accurate to describe this approach as one which re-trains the nervous system moreso than the muscular system. Given that the nervous system develops a significant set of problems in people with low back pain, we need to focus our treatment on this nervous system error.

Transversus abdominis (TrA) is the deepest of the four abdominal muscles. It is built like a corset around the trunk and is the only abdominal muscle which attaches to our spinal joints. It is normally the first muscle our nervous system activates during any type of movement.

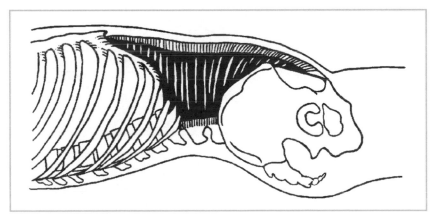

Transversus Abdominus (TrA) - the only abdominal muscle which attaches directly to our spinal joints

To develop an isolated TrA contraction, we actually make use of an odd neurologic link between TrA and the *pelvic floor* muscles. Our TrA activates quite nicely, and independently of the other abdominal muscles, when we gently contract the front part of our pelvic floor muscle. If you are a woman who has done the *Kegel* exercise before, you'll know what I'm referring to (actually, both men and women have pelvic floor muscles, but women will generally be more familiar with them as the *Kegel* is a common post- childbirth exercise).

To activate the transversus via the pelvic floor, lay down in a comfortable, pain-free position in a quiet room where you can concentrate on your exercises. Carefully, gently and very gradually, contract what is known as your pelvic floor muscle. To gently contract the pelvic floor, imagine having to urinate but needing to control your bladder (imagine a long line at the movie theater washroom after *Schindler's List* and a pair of extra-large *Diet-Cokes*); to do this, we use our pelvic floor muscle. More specific imagery, however, may be helpful.

Both men and women may visualize the pelvic floor muscle as a hammock strung between the tailbone and the pubic bone in front. When the pelvic floor is relaxed, it is like a relaxed hammock. Try to tighten the hammock, especially its front half, drawing it gently upwards or inwards and making it firmer. For the men specifically, imagine that your testicles sit outside your groin but at the open ends of two tunnels that begin deep in the body. Try to gently draw the testicles back 'inside' through the tunnels. Gradually draw the pelvic floor inwards while continuing to breath in a relaxed, easy manner.

For the women, if you're comfortable with the use of tampons, insert a tampon as you normally would. Then using your pelvic floor/vaginal muscles, gently grip the tampon from 'inside'. If you would rather not use a tampon, try using the same imagery without the tampon. With a few days practice, both men and women should be able to consistently activate the front half of their pelvic floor.

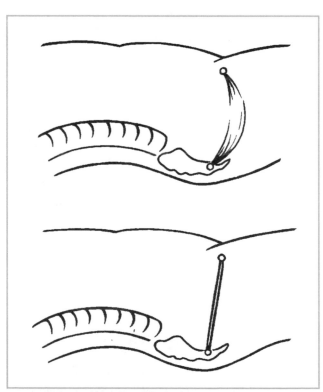

Once you have a good ability to activate the pelvic floor, begin to pay attention to the TrA muscle. Laying on your back with your knees bent and your fingers positioned as in the picture on page 45, carefully activate your pelvic floor - feel for a very gentle firmness developing under your finger tips. If TrA activates correctly, you'll feel a subtle tensioning of the muscle under your fingers *without the feeling that a muscle is bulging up into your fingers*. Just to add to the mental challenge, you must be able to breathe quietly and normally while holding these gentle contractions of TrA.

The position of the pelvic floor when laying on our back. It may be thought of as a muscular hammock between the tailbone and the front of the pelvis. The upper figure shows a relaxed pelvic floor. A gentle, inward contraction of the pelvic floor will activate the transversus abdomonis muscle.

The initial transversus activation is usually performed in a back-lying position. The finger tips - positioned just inside the 'front corners' of the pelvis - are used to feel for the very subtle activation or firmness which develops in TrA as we contract our pelvic floor.

The objective of this technique is gaining an isolated activation of the TrA. The ability to voluntarily activate just the TrA (and in stage two, just the TrA and the multifidus together) seems to be the key to correcting the nervous system's problems with these important muscles. A very gentle activation is needed in order to activate the TrA in isolation, to prevent the other abdominals from contracting as well.

Key Pointers to Help with Your TrA Activation ...

1. choose a quiet, distraction-free space to do your exercises and lie down in a comfortable position; if on your back, keep your knees bent and slightly apart; if on your side, place a pillow between your knees

2. during each session, plan to work for a maximum of ten minutes ... it is difficult to maintain our concentration on something so challenging for longer than this

3. work for short periods but as frequently as your schedule permits (two or three sessions per day should be a minimum - five or six is great)

4. if after a few minutes of successful practice you are no longer able to 'get it', the muscles are likely tired - stop at this point and try again later

5. to confirm that other abdominal muscles are remaining quiet, place one hand on your lower rib cage near the bottom of your breast bone - any muscles under this hand should stay relaxed as you activate TrA

6. while it is often more convenient to practice in a sitting posture, this will not work well for us at this stage; any upright posture requires many muscles to activate and thus we don't get the precise isolation of TrA that we require

Stage Two - The Combined TrA & Multifidus Activation

The importance of learning to activate the multifidus along with the TrA cannot be overstated. My interpretation of the research as well as my clinical experience with patients has convinced me that when people get correct control of both TrA and multifidus they have a very high likelihood of gaining complete control of their back pain. The research regarding this approach has noted that, on average, by the sixth week of training, people who have good isolated control of transversus and multifidus will have corrected the size deficit involving the multifidus muscle.

The fact that the multifidus re-gains its normal size with this exercise is strong evidence for the suggestion that this approach corrects the nervous system error which was responsible for the loss of the muscle's size in the first place. The only way we know of to achieve this is to gain isolated voluntary control over the muscle. Without this, the overall approach will be much less successful.

The problem at this stage is that it is very difficult to do this part of the program on your own. A health care professional skilled in this technique will be able to identify the specific spinal level at which your spine is unstable, and thus the precise segment of the multifidus which needs to be re-trained. Ultimately this will result in a more efficient and successful therapeutic process.

If that is simply not an option, a good friend or significant other will be your only other choice. Since some readers will not have access to a health care professional who is familiar with this approach, I will discuss it in some detail. If you are able to work with a professional, follow their instructions carefully. Their method might vary a little from the one described here. There is some room built in to the approach for individual preference and clinical judgement.

Assuming you are working with a friend, lie on your side or your belly, whichever is more comfortable. If you can lie on your belly without back pain, place a pillow or two under your abdomen. Have your partner place the tips of their thumbs gently, but with a degree of careful firmness, into the multifidus muscle close to the spinal column (note the outline of the multifidus muscle drawn on this patient). If your partner has especially sensitive hands they might be able to locate the region of multifidus which is smaller - it will feel 'mushy'. If so, they should place their thumbs at this level. The comfortable sense of their thumbs in your multifidus will make it a little easier for you to activate the muscle.

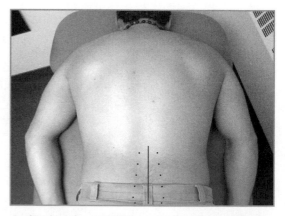

Activating the multifidus; your partner should place their thumbs on either side of the spine and towards the lower third of the muscle.

Beginning with an easy breath in, exhale and gradually activate your pelvic floor and TrA as in your previous exercises. Maintain that contraction and shift your attention to the multifidus and the comfortable feeling of your helper's thumbs in the muscle. Think of squeezing or drawing the multifidus muscle together, towards the center of the spinal column just as you would if you were squeezing your buttocks together (keep your buttocks relaxed though - this imagery is for the multifidus only).

You will initially have a very hard time feeling even the slightest activity in the multifidus especially if you keep your remaining abdominal, low back and buttocks muscles quiet. As with TrA, work for short periods with frequent rest breaks. This exercise is very difficult to do and your brain will become tired with the effort. Once you can no longer concentrate - stop. Trying to force it to happen never works. You must find a way to work at this while relaxed and in a positive frame of mind.

If you have a health care professional to work with, they may well have various monitoring devices for you to use which can help you to know if you are really activating the multifidus muscle. Regardless of their preferences, you must learn to gently turn on the pelvic floor, TrA and multifidus as a group, and keep all other muscles perfectly relaxed. You must also be able to breathe quietly and gently while you hold the activation.

Please take as long as is necessary to accomplish this objective. Feel free to try other postures such as side lying or back lying although in these positions it will be harder for your helper to find and feel your multifidus. If you are working with a professional, they will be able to accomodate any position you want to try to work in. The same pointers detailed previously for TrA also apply to the combination TrA & multifidus activation.

Stage Two - The Combined TrA & Multifidus Activation
Primary Objectives:

1. contract TrA and multifidus together without *any other muscles* activating at the same time

2. maintain an easy breathing pattern while holding the TrA and multifidus contraction

3. hold each isolated TrA and multifidus contraction for ten seconds, and be able to perform ten of these with ideal technique in a row

4. once you are able to do this consistently and perfectly in one position, try it in the other lying-down postures as well - just like your first attempts at the TrA activation, each new posture will seem very difficult at first

Stage Three - Challenging the Combined TrA & Multifidus Activation

Once you're able to perform a perfectly isolated TrA and multifidus contraction, hold it for ten seconds ten times and maintain an easy breathing pattern, you are ready to move on to stage three. Congratulations - having made it to this point, you have gotten through the most difficult part of the entire process. Everything from this point forward will seem relatively simple.

Now that TrA and multifidus are reasonably well controlled you will need to begin challenging these muscles in a gradual but progressive fashion. At this point the idea is to carefully challenge these muscles to do exactly what they are designed to do - stabilize the trunk while we move our arms or legs in some way.

Stage three exercises require you to maintain your TrA and multifidus activation, then slowly move an arm or a leg or, an arm and leg, in such a way that it is more difficult for your nervous system to keep your TrA and multifidus activated. At the same time, it is now appropriate to add some deep layer, position sensing exercises.

You may now follow the exercise photos on the next few pages along with the instructions of your therapist as you progress. Keep in mind that it is still important to maintain a good TrA and multifidus activation and to breathe easily during these exercises.

Stage Three ... Therapeutic Dynamic Middle Layer Exercises

At this point in your rehabilitation program it is necessary to begin training these muscles to actually stabilize the spinal joints while your arms and legs are in motion. To do this correctly you must maintain a steady activation of transversus and multifidus, breathe gently and prevent your pelvis from rocking side to side or backwards and forwards.

As you do these exercises, you may feel some **small** amount of tension develop in other abdominal or low back muscles; this is to be expected at this stage. However, you should not need to fully contract your abdominals or hold your breath in order to perform them.

You should NOT feel any pain whatsoever while performing these exercises. Pain is not a good thing nor is it something which must be worked through to get better!

Maintain your attention on your transversus/multifidus activation as you do these exercises. The act of moving your leg to the side or reaching an arm overhead does not demand your attention at this point. Keep your concentration centered on the transversus and multifidus - maintain a steady, even tension in these muscles throughout the exercise. Only move the leg (or arm) as far as you are able, while still maintaining a perfect activation of transversus and multifidus. The amount of leg movement is not important; only that you can move the leg and maintain good control of transversus and multifidus.

Stage Three ... Therapeutic Dynamic Middle Layer Exercises

Perform only as many repetitions as you can without pain and while maintaining excellent technique!

1   bent knee fall out

• maintain TrA & MF contraction while letting knee move slowly outwards toward floor; alternate legs

* use your finger tips to monitor tension in the lower abdomen - if you feel this tension drop as you move your leg, do not move the leg further - only move your hip within a range of motion through which you can keep TrA & MF contracted

* use your hands to monitor the position of your pelvis as the leg moves - the pelvis should stay perfectly still

* maintain an easy breathing pattern throughout

* when you can do ten repetitions well, you may move on to exercise 2

2   heel slide

• maintain TrA & MF contraction while sliding foot away slowly along floor; alternate legs

* same instructions as in exercise 1 above

* when you can do ten repetitions well, you may move on to exercise 3

3   slow arms reaching over head

• maintain TrA & MF contraction while letting arms move slowly overhead toward floor

* if you notice that the tension in your TrA or MF drop as you move your arms, do not move further - only move your arms as far as you are able to keep your TrA & MF contracted

* maintain an easy breathing pattern throughout

Note:

The small open boxes beside each picture are intended to help therapists indicate to their patients which exercises are to be performed. Simply place a checkmark in the box corresponding to the intended exercise.

Stage Three ... Therapeutic Dynamic Middle Layer Exercises

Perform only as many repetitions as you can without pain and while maintaining excellent technique!

4   single knee lift

- maintain TrA & MF contraction while lifting thigh carefully toward your shoulder
- **this is a difficult exercise** ... it will take some practice to maintain your TrA & MF activation and lift a foot off the floor - as simple as this sounds it is, in fact, very hard to do correctly

* use your finger tips to monitor tension in the lower abdomen - if you feel this tension drop as you move your leg, do not move the leg further - move only so far as you can while maintaining a good contraction in transversus and multifidus

5   single knee lift and opposite arm overhead reach

The 'dying bug' exercise ...

- maintain TrA & MF contraction while lifting one thigh and raising the opposite arm overhead
- not too difficult once you have mastered exercises 3 and 4

Therapeutic Middle Layer Exercises ...

The therapeutic middle layer exercises presented here are those we use daily with patients. Most patients should recognize a significant improvement in their back pain by the time they are able to do exercises 1 - 3 well. Interestingly, patients rarely need to perform exercises 4 or 5 in order to control their back pain. These seem to border on conditioning exercises and thus provide a nice transition into a conditioning program for those who desire greater core strength once their back pain is under control.

Stage Three ... Deep Layer Exercises

These exercises are intended to improve the 'position-sensing' function of the spine's deep layer. At this point it is necessary to define certain terms used to describe the performance of these exercises.

Base of Support

The distance between two or more parts of your body which are in contact with a supporting surface such as the floor. For example, when you stand with your feet spread shoulder width apart, you have a wider base of support than when you stand with your feet together. A wider base of support is a more stable base of support; a more narrow base of support is a less stable base of support.

Points of Stable Contact

The number of connections we have through our body to a stable surface. For example, standing with two feet on the ground provides two stable points of contact. Sitting on a ball with only one foot on the floor provides only one stable point of contact while kneeling on a ball provides no stable point of contact.

Stage Three ... Therapeutic Deep Layer Exercises

Perform only as many repetitions as you can without pain and while maintaining excellent technique!

1   Ball Sitting

- eyes open, wide base of support
- practice maintaining balance while holding a transversus & multifidus contraction
- try to sit for up to 5 minutes while holding this contraction for up to 30 seconds then resting for 30 seconds
- sit tall, feeling as though your lower back is held gently in its natural curve

NOTE - tips on ball selection, correct sizing and the inflation of stability balls is found on page 108

Stage Three ... Therapeutic Deep Layer Exercises

Perform only as many repetitions as you can without pain and while maintaining excellent technique!

2   **Ball Sitting**

- eyes open, narrow base of support
- hold a transversus & multifidus contraction
- try to sit for up to 5 minutes while holding this contraction for up to 30 seconds then resting for 30 seconds
- sit tall, feeling as though your lower back is held gently in its natural curve

3   **Ball Sitting**

- eyes closed, wide base of support
- contract TrA and MF; hold as in exercises 1 and 2

4   **Ball Sitting**

- eyes closed, narrow base of support
- contract TrA and MF; hold as in exercises 1 and 2

Stage Three ... Therapeutic Deep Layer Exercises

Perform only as many repetitions as you can without pain and while maintaining excellent technique!

5   Ball Sitting

- eyes open, narrow base of support with arm movements
- hold a transversus & multifidus contraction
- try to sit for up to 5 minutes while holding this contraction for up to 30 seconds then resting for 30 seconds
- sit tall, feeling as though your lower back is held gently in its natural curve

- the type of arm motions you use are less important than is the maintenance of the TrA and MF activation and a natural low back posture

6   Ball Sitting

- eyes closed, narrow base of support with arm movements
- contract TrA and MF; hold as in exercise 5

- the type of arm motions you use are less important than is the maintenance of the TrA and MF activation and a natural low back posture

7   Ball Sitting

- eyes closed, one point of stable contact, with arm movements
- contract TrA and MF; hold as in exercise 5

- the type of arm and leg motions you use are less important than is the maintenance of the TrA and MF activation and a natural low back posture

Transitioning From a Therapeutic Stabilization Program to a Conditioning Program

Many readers will now have excellent control and activation of their key middle layer muscles and will have noted a significant improvement in their back pain. For some they will have achieved what they set out to do; others will want to progress their exercises further, moving in a direction of conditioning or training as opposed to maintaining their therapeutic exercise program.

If you wish to continue with your current exercises, follow your health care professional's advice as to how frequently you should perform your program. Some people will need to maintain their therapeutic exercises on a daily basis, others will be able to cut back to only two or three times each week. Some readers will need to continue with their therapeutic exercises indefinitely, others for only a few weeks or months. Ideally, you'll be able to incorporate these exercises into your daily or weekly routine and continue with them.

For those who wish to transition into the conditioning program, carefully follow the instructions in the next sections of the book. A health care professional will be able to assist you in the transition from the therapeutic to the conditioning exercises. If you've had back pain and now want to move into the conditioning exercises, try to maintain your TrA and multifidus activation with each of the exercises you use.

Book II

Chapter 6
Essential Concepts in Stabilization-based Conditioning

Ideally, each person's stabilization-based conditioning program should be a unique exercise *prescription* since the physical activity demands and injury history of each person will be unique. While providing the same generic program for all people with, for example, a previous lumbar disc injury may at first seem reasonable, this approach does not lead to success as readily as does a more 'person specific' program.

To illustrate this point, let's say that a 36 year-old airline pilot who was once a competitive figure skater and a 58 year-old accounts manager with no athletic background have each recovered from a spinal disc injury. They have rehabilitated their transversus and multifidus muscles via the Australian method of therapeutic spinal stabilization as described in chapter five and are ready to begin a conditioning program.

The pilot now competes in triathalons while the accounts manager prefers walking for exercise. Given their different occupations and physical activity interests, they will obviously have different physical demands placed on their spinal column and therefore their conditioning programs should be more tailored to their individual needs.

Instead of presenting a 'post-rehabilitation cookbook' with the same collection of recipes for everyone, several important concepts will be outlined which should be considered when following a stabilization-based conditioning program. People with previous back problems should consult with a physical therapist to design the safest and most effective program based on their type of injury, stage of recovery and their current physical ability. They will need to re-establish correct middle layer muscle function before beginning these exercises. If you have a healthy, non-painful back, you may wish to put together your own program based on these concepts or you may wish to consult with a licensed physical therapist familiar with stabilization training.

Integrative Training

The exercises described in Book II combine middle and outer layer muscle functions and will progressively challenge you from balance, stability and muscular performance perspectives. They require the spinal joints plus varying combinations of ankle, knee, hip, shoulder, elbow and wrist joints, and all the muscles which function at these joints, to work together to perform a given exercise. They require us to support our body weight, stabilize our core, move our arms or legs and in some cases, lift heavy weights, all at the same time. To an extent not seen with traditional conditioning programs, these exercises simultaneously train our joint, muscular and nervous systems for optimal performance.

As such, these exercises are extremely effective at training the body to perform 'real-life' activities (this is discussed in greater depth in chapter nine). Whether a person's real-life involves carrying the groceries into the house, transferring patients from wheelchairs to hospital beds or hitting a golf ball 300 yards, everyday activities require the body to work in this integrated fashion. For this reason, along with the fact that the phrase *stabilization-based conditioning exercises* seems a bit awkward, from this point forward these exercises will be referred to as *Integrative Training* exercises, or IT exercises.

To begin, we'll define some of the terms used throughout the next few sections.

Deep Layer Exercises

Exercises which develop position sense through our spine and extremities. These usually challenge our ability to maintain our balance in some way.

Middle Layer Exercises

Exercises which train the key stabilization muscles of the trunk. The middle layer muscles include transversus abdominis (TrA), quadratus lumborum (QL) and multifidus (MF). The middle layer exercises are further divided into two groups - *static and dynamic*.

Static middle layer Integrative Training exercises are those which require us to hold a certain position or posture without movement. *Dynamic* middle layer Integrative Training exercises require us to create movement somewhere in our body while maintaining a stable trunk or core.

Outer Layer Exercises

These exercises develop the power muscles of the trunk. People who play very physical sports such as hockey, football and rugby or who have very physically demanding jobs (e.g., forestry workers, firefighters) may need to spend more time on these exercises than people with more sedentary lives or whose sports are not quite as hard on the body.

Base of Support

The distance between two or more parts of your body which are in contact with a supporting surface such as the floor. For example, when you stand with your feet spread shoulder width apart, you have a wider base of support than when you stand with your feet together. Standing on only one foot reduces your base of support to the area under your foot. A wider base of support is a more stable base of support; a more narrow base of support is a less stable base of support.

Points of Stable Contact

The number of connections we have through our body to a stable surface. For example, standing with two feet on the ground provides two stable points of contact. Standing on one foot provides only one stable point of contact while kneeling on a large ball provides no stable point of contact. Kneeling on a large ball while holding on to a wall with one hand provides a single point of stable contact.

Essential Integrative Training Concepts

Concept 1:

Integrative Training or IT exercises and general daily activities should not exceed a person's stabilization ability.

Researchers have determined that spinal injury occurs when the muscles of the spine are no longer able to stabilize the joints of the spinal column; therefore, it is imperative that people perform exercises which do not overwhelm the capabilities of their stabilizing muscles. This is true of both IT exercises and other daily activities. For example, a person with a moderate degree of stabilizing ability may be able to tolerate a brisk walk for aerobic exercise but they may not be able to stabilize their spine while jogging. Likewise, a injured worker may be sufficiently stable to perform a lifting activity involving 10 kg loads but not 15 kg loads.

When we perform exercises or physical activities which overwhelm our middle layer's stabilization ability, the body will use the outer layer muscles as stabilizers. Because these large movement muscles are not designed for stabilization functions, this often leads to further mechanical problems and increased pain. This represents a faulty movement pattern and should be avoided whenever possible.

Essential Integrative Training Concepts

Concept 2:

Quality of movement before quantity of movement.

The overall goal of Integrative Training is to teach our body to make correct use of the deep, middle and outer layer muscles. To achieve this goal, we must perform the exercises with an emphasis on technique rather than a high number of repetitions. Similarly, exercises which are too difficult for us (see Concept 1) will create too significant a challenge for our stabilization muscles and will cause our body to compensate by excessively activating the outer layer muscles in an attempt to meet the stability demands of the exercise.

As tempting as it may be to progress through the exercise levels quickly, please be sure that you are completely capable of performing each exercise correctly before moving to more challenging variations.

Concept 3:

Start with simple exercises and gradually add more challenging exercises as your technique permits.

Begin by performing exercises emphasizing position sense and static stability (the deep and middle layer exercises) separately. When you become good at each of these, move onto exercises which combine position sense and static stability challenges in a single exercise. This involves holding a posture while on a SwissBall or wobble board. Finally, combine position sense and dynamic stability exercises for the greatest degree of challenge.

Concept 4:

Position sense or deep layer exercises are progressed (i.e., made more challenging) by decreasing the base of support and the number of points of stable contact.

As defined earlier, the base of support refers to the distance between your feet or hands on the floor during exercises. The same exercise performed with a wide base of support will be more difficult if performed with a more narrow base of support. The number of points of stable contact refers to the total number of hands or feet you have in contact with a stable surface (usually the floor) during any exercise. An exercise performed easily with three points of stable contact will be more difficult when attempted with only a single point of stable contact.

Position sense (deep layer) exercises may also be progressed by closing your eyes or by adding movement to the exercise. Most people are quite dependent on their vision to help

Essential Integrative Training Concepts

maintain their balance; therefore, we can make the deep layer exercises much more difficult by performing the exercise with our eyes closed. In fact, any exercise performed with the eyes closed allows us to be more aware of our body and how it is moving or working.

Of course, exercising with the eyes closed should only be attempted if there is no risk of injury should you lose your ability to maintain the position. For example, many athletes are able to kneel on a large inflatable ball as a form of advanced deep layer training. If the person closes their eyes they will make the exercise much more difficult, but they will also be at higher risk of falling off the ball.

Deep layer position sense exercises may also be progressed by attempting to maintain our balance while moving our arms or legs.

Concept 5 - Part 1:
Static IT exercises are progressed by holding each posture for longer periods of time while performing fewer repetitions

A static IT exercise is an exercise where we attempt to maintain a certain position or posture to train for endurance in the spinal stabilizers. At first, we might perform ten repetitions of the exercise, holding the position each time for five to ten seconds. To progress these, we would hold each position for longer periods of time, up to 30 or 45 seconds. As the length of time spent holding each position increases, the number of repetitions may decrease. Therefore we may begin doing a certain static IT exercise 10 times, holding each posture for 10 seconds. As the endurance of these muscles improves we might perform only three or four repetitions, but we would be holding each posture for up to 45 seconds.

A good measure of how long to hold each posture involves movement quality; hold each position for as long as you can maintain near-perfect technique. If you begin to lose optimal technique after ten seconds, perform a higher number of repetitions, stopping when your technique begins to fail. As your endurance improves, you will find yourself holding positions for longer periods of time. As this happens, perform fewer repetitions.

Concept 5 - Part 2:
Dynamic IT exercises are progressed by performing more repetitions

Dynamic IT exercises require us to move in some way while maintaining a stable trunk or core. These exercises are progressed by performing more repetitions. Again, the key consideration is technique. Perform as many repetitions of a given dynamic IT exercise as

---

Essential Integrative Training Concepts

you can until your technique begins to falter. When you have done several repetitions and can no longer do the exercise with perfect form, stop. If you find yourself performing more than twenty repetitions of a given dynamic IT exercise with excellent technique, it may be time to move on to a more challenging exercise.

Concept 6

Avoid any exercise which increases your back or neck pain.

In chapter 1 we discussed the fact that following spinal injury, the body often responds by 'shutting down' the stabilization muscles near the site of the injury. This occurs via two similar but distinct mechanisms.

Researchers have shown that when swelling (fluid) builds up within a joint, the stabilizing muscle of that joint stops working. For example, at a large joint like the knee, the quadriceps muscle will start to have difficulty contracting with as little as one tablespoon (15 - 20 ml) of fluid within the joint. With almost any form of acute joint injury, including spinal injury, there will be some amount of swelling within the joint. Unfortunately, where there is joint swelling, there is muscle deactivation, usually affecting the middle layer muscles at the injured joint.

The other mechanism which appears to lead to this deactivation of stabilizing muscle involves pain. Less is known about the process by which pain causes a 'shutting-down' of stabilizing muscle; however, it is a common problem, especially in the acute stage of an injury.

Since pain will often deactivate the stabilizing, middle layer muscles we wish to re-train, it is important that a person with back pain begin with the therapeutic stabilization exercises detailed in Book I. Under no circumstances is it beneficial to push our exercises to the point of pain, especially in the therapeutic phase. If a given exercise makes the pain worse, modify the exercise or perform some other exercise in its place which serves a similar purpose (i.e., position sense, stabilization or powerful movement). If this doesn't help, seek advice from a physical therapist.

Concept 7

Ideally, people with previous low back pain should perform their IT exercises while maintaining a contraction of the transversus abdominis and multifidus muscles.

A large amount of anatomical, biomechanical and neurophysiological research has identified that the TrA and multifidus muscles play very important roles in low back stabilization.

Essential Integrative Training Concepts

Many physical therapists now appreciate that proper function of the TrA and multifidus is the key to lumbar stabilization. Further studies have found that when we move an arm or leg (as when we are walking, reaching, kicking, etc.) the nervous system activates the TrA and multifidus *before* the actual arm or leg muscles which produce the limb movement. The TrA and multifidus are used by the body to stabilize the lower spine so that movement of the arms and legs can occur more efficiently and without placing undue stress on the spine itself.

Chapter five in Book I described the techniques used to re-activate and train the TrA and multifidus muscles. People with back pain or who have had any episodes of significant low back pain in the past five years should begin with the therapeutic exercises in Book I before moving to those in Book II.

An ongoing question at this point is whether people who have never had low back pain need to consciously activate their TrA and multifidus when performing IT exercises. The research at this time suggests that if a person has enjoyed a healthy spine, their middle layer muscles should work properly. This would seem to indicate that there would be no benefit to having these people learn to voluntarily activate their TrA and multifidus, that they should just go ahead and perform the exercises and let their properly functioning system look after things. Others have suggested that even with a healthy system, there may be a back injury prevention benefit from learning to activate these muscles as per the techniques in chapter five.

As there are no real answers to this question as yet, it is likely best left to the individual to decide for themselves. If you feel more confident performing the IT exercises while maintaining a voluntary contraction of TrA and multifidus then practice the therapeutic exercises as previously described in chapter five before proceeding to the IT exercises in Book II.

Concept 8
Have fun with your exercise program!

When was the last time you met someone who just couldn't wait to do their abdominal exercises? Even the most enthusiastic exercise nut still dreads the thought of doing endless sit-ups, crunches and oblique twists. Many more people have given up altogether because they find their neck or lower back hurts when they do these old-style exercises. The fact that an up-to-date IT program is based on better and more reliable science is reason enough to try it. That people actually *enjoy* this approach is certainly unique when it comes to abdominal exercises.

Essential Integrative Training Concepts

The fact that Integrative Training often seems more like play than exercise means that people are much more likely to stick with their exercise program. As people move into the moderate level exercises and begin using the large, inflatable 'swissballs', the little kid in each of us quickly recognizes the fun side to integrative training.

Concept 9

Begin gradually and add more exercise days as you become comfortable with the program.

If you have not exercised regularly for some time, it is a good idea to begin with one or two exercise days each week, and gradually add more exercise sessions as both your normal daily routine and your body adjust to the new activity. Many new exercisers 'jump right in' with a three, four or five day-a-week exercise program, only to 'burn out' quickly. Many of us will need some time to see how the rest of our life is going to cope with our new exercise program. Likewise, our body may need some time to adjust to our new level of physical activity. Start slowly, build gradually and your chances of sticking with the program will be much greater!

Chapter 7
Integrative Training: The Complete Exercise Program

A physical therapist will be very helpful in planning your exercise program based on your injury history, the type of sport you play and your current stabilization ability. One or two exercises from each category (deep layer, middle layer and outer layer) should be included in your program. At all times, follow the instructions of your physical therapist and the basic concepts discussed in chapter six.

When designing your program, choose exercises which *challenge* as opposed to *overwhelm* your current stabilization ability. An exercise is too advanced for your present stabilization potential if it causes pain or if you are unable to hold the posture for at least five seconds using excellent technique.

Once you have progressed to the exercises which make use of the SwissBall, you must remember to use a certain amount of caution and common sense. Exercises of any kind which are performed using these very unstable pieces of exercise equipment may lead to serious injury if you fall or lose your balance. Perform your SwissBall exercises in an open area away from objects which could cause injury if you were to fall off the ball. Work with a reliable spotter when performing exercises which create a significant challenge to your balance or which could potentially cause injury if you were to lose your balance.

Lastly, use a burst-resistant ball, especially if you are lifting weights while on the ball, to minimize your risk of serious injury should the ball be punctured. Burst-resistant balls are not puncture proof, but they are designed to deflate slowly should a hole develop in the ball.

Note:
The small open boxes beside each picture are intended to help therapists indicate to their patients which exercises are to be performed at a given point in their IT programs. Simply place a checkmark in the box corresponding to the intended exercise. Using pencil is a good idea as the exercises used will likely change over time.

Deep Layer / Position Sense Exercises

These progress from easier to harder, therefore Deep Layer exercise 7 is typically more challenging than is Deep Layer exercise number 3. If you've had back problems, maintain a good transversus and multifidus contraction throughout and try to hold each posture a few seconds longer every day.

1 Single Leg Standing

- with / without additional point of stable contact
- start by holding for a few seconds then build to 30 seconds
- when you can easily hold this position for 20 seconds, begin trying exercise 2, below

- *always stand on a slightly bent knee*

2 Single Leg Standing

- eyes closed
- as with exercise 1, begin with a few seconds and gradually build to 30 seconds
- when you can easily hold this position for 20 seconds, begin trying exercise 3, below

3 Single Leg Standing

- eyes closed with arm movements
- begin with slow easy, symmetrical arm movements
- progress by moving the arms in different directions and at various speeds

Deep Layer / Position Sense Exercises

Progressing from easier to harder ... if you've had back problems, maintain the transversus and multifidus contraction throughout; hold each posture a few seconds longer every day.

4   Ball Sitting

- eyes open, wide base of support

- if using a TrA & MF contraction, try to sit for up to 5 minutes while maintaining this contraction for up to 30 seconds then resting for 30 seconds

- sit tall, feeling as though your lower back is held gently in its natural curve

5   Ball Sitting

- eyes open, narrow base of support

- same instructions as in the above exercise

6   Ball Sitting

- eyes closed, wide base of support

- same instructions as in exercise 4

Deep Layer / Position Sense Exercises

Progressing from easier to harder ... if you've had back problems, maintain the transversus and multifidus contraction throughout; hold each posture a few seconds longer every day.

7   Ball Sitting

- eyes closed, narrow base of support

- if using a TrA & multifidus contraction, try to sit for up to 5 minutes while maintaining this contraction for up to 30 seconds then resting for 30 seconds

- sit tall, feeling as though your lower back is held gently in its natural curve

8   Ball Sitting

- eyes open, narrow base of support with arm movements

- instructions as in above exercise

9   Ball Sitting

- eyes closed, narrow base of support with arm movements

- instructions as per exercise 7

Deep Layer / Position Sense Exercises

Progressing from easier to harder ... if you've had back problems, maintain the transversus and multifidus contraction throughout; hold each posture a few seconds longer every day.

10   **Ball Sitting**

- eyes open, one point of stable contact

- if using a TrA & multifidus contraction, try to sit for up to 5 minutes while maintaining this contraction for up to 30 seconds then resting for 30 seconds

- sit tall, feeling as though your lower back is held gently in its natural curve

11   **Ball Sitting**

- eyes open, one point of stable contact, with arm movements

- instructions as in above exercise

12   **Ball Sitting**

- eyes closed, one point of stable contact

- instructions as in exercise 10

Deep Layer / Position Sense Exercises

Progressing from easier to harder ... if you've had back problems, maintain the transversus and multifidus contraction throughout; hold each posture a few seconds longer every day.

13 Ball Sitting

- eyes closed, one point of stable contact, with arm movements

- if using a TrA & multifidus contraction, try to sit for up to 5 minutes while maintaining this contraction for up to 30 seconds then resting for 30 seconds

- sit tall, feeling as though your lower back is held gently in its natural curve

14 Ball Sitting

- no point of stable contact

- instructions as in above exercise

15 Ball Sitting

- no point of stable contact, add arm movements

- instructions as in exercise13

Deep Layer / Position Sense Exercises

Progressing from easier to harder ... if you've had back problems, maintain the transversus and multifidus contraction throughout; hold each posture a few seconds longer every day.

16   Ball Sitting

- eyes closed & no point of stable contact

- if using a TrA & multifidus contraction, try to sit for up to 5 minutes while maintaining this contraction for up to 30 seconds then resting for 30 seconds

- sit tall, feeling as though your lower back is held gently in its natural curve

17   Ball Sitting

- no point of stable contact, eyes closed, add arm movements

- instructions as in above exercise

18   Ball Kneeling

- two points of stable contact, eyes open

Hint:
To get up into a kneeling position on the ball, stand with the ball in front of you, resting between your knees. Your arms are reaching forward with your finger tips just touching the edge of the chair back. From this position, slowly roll up onto the ball, holding onto the chair back as soon as you begin to roll forward. As always, make sure someone is close by acting as a 'spotter'. Remember - do not use a chair which is on wheels as your 'stable' point of contact!

Deep Layer / Position Sense Exercises

Progressing from easier to harder ... if you've had back problems, maintain the transversus and multifidus contraction throughout; hold each posture a few seconds longer every day.

19   Ball Kneeling

- two points of stable contact, eyes closed

- if using a TrA & multifidus contraction, try to kneel for 3 to 5 minutes while maintaining this contraction

20   Ball Kneeling

- one point of stable contact, eyes open

- if using a TrA & multifidus contraction, try to kneel for 3 to 5 minutes while maintaining this contraction

21   Ball Kneeling

- one point of stable contact, eyes closed

- if using a TrA & multifidus contraction, try to kneel for 3 to 5 minutes while maintaining this contraction

Deep Layer / Position Sense Exercises

Progressing from easier to harder ... if you've had back problems, maintain the transversus and multifidus contraction throughout; hold each posture a few seconds longer every day.

22   **Ball Kneeling**

- no points of stable contact, eyes open

- if using a TrA & multifidus contraction, try to kneel for 3 to 5 minutes while maintaining this contraction

23   **Ball Kneeling**

- no points of stable contact, eyes open, add arm movement

- if using a TrA & multifidus contraction, try to kneel for 3 to 5 minutes while maintaining this contraction

24   **Ball Kneeling**

- no points of stable contact, eyes open, add trunk movement such as twists and side bends

- if using a TrA & multifidus contraction, try to kneel for 3 to 5 minutes while maintaining this contraction

Deep Layer / Position Sense Exercises

Progressing from easier to harder ... if you've had back problems, maintain the transversus and multifidus contraction throughout; hold each posture a few seconds longer every day.

25 Ball Kneeling

- no points of stable contact, eyes closed
- the eyes closed option makes these VERY difficult to do!

- if using a TrA & multifidus contraction, try to kneel for 3 to 5 minutes while maintaining this contraction

26 Ball Kneeling

- no points of stable contact, eyes closed, with arm movements

- if using a TrA & multifidus contraction, try to kneel for 3 to 5 minutes while maintaining this contraction

27 Ball Standing

- from a safety perspective this is not an exercise for everyone
- **bones get broken, shoulders get dislocated and skulls get cracked open attempting this exercise**

- for a *very small percentage* of athletes, there is value in taking the deep layer exercises to this level

- the safest way to begin this exercise is to place the ball at the base of a tricep dip rack, as in the picture
- you may then lower yourself on to the ball, while keeping a handhold close by
- as you become more comfortable, take your hands off the bar for brief periods - a few seconds - until you develop a feel for the standing position

DO NOT ATTEMPT THIS WITHOUT A RELIABLE SPOTTER CLOSE BY AT ALL TIMES

Middle Layer Stabilization Exercises

The middle layer exercises are organized into three sections: 1) transversus abdominis/multifidus exercises; 2) static middle layer exercises and 3) dynamic middle layer exercises. Within each section, all exercises progress from easier to harder. If you have had low back problems in the past you must develop good control of the transversus and multifidus muscles before beginning these exercises (see chapter five).

Transversus Abdominis & Multifidus - Advanced Training

1   Basic TrA & MF activation

• this series of exercises will be most helpful for people with a history of low back pain as they will need to fully train the transversus and multifidus muscles prior to attempting the static and dynamic middle layer exercises

• contract pelvic floor (see instructions which begin on page 43) and activate both TrA and MF together - hold for 10 to 15 seconds and repeat 15 times

• people with a healthy lower back may consider activation of the pelvic floor/ TrA/multifidus as an option

2   TrA & MF - bent knee fall out

• maintain TrA & MF contraction while letting knee move slowly outwards toward floor; alternate legs

* use your finger tips to monitor tension in the lower abdomen - if you feel this tension drop as you move your leg, do not move the leg further - only move your hip within a range of motion through which you can keep TrA & MF contracted
* use your hands to monitor the position of your pelvis as the leg moves - the pelvis should stay perfectly still
* maintain an easy breathing pattern throughout
* when you can do ten repetitions well, you may move on to exercise 3

3   TrA & MF - heel slide

• maintain TrA & MF contraction while sliding one foot away slowly along floor; alternate legs

* same rules about hip and pelvis movement and muscle tension in TrA & MF - if you feel the pelvis tilt or the muscle tension drop, do not move the hip any further

Middle Layer Stabilization Exercises

Transversus Abdominis & Multifidus - Advanced Training

4   **TrA & MF - arms reaching over head**

- maintain TrA & MF contraction while letting arms move overhead toward floor

* if you feel the tension in your TrA & MF drop as you move your arms, do not move further - only move your arms as far as you are able to keep your middle layer contracted

5   **TrA & MF - single knee lift**

- maintain TrA & MF contraction while bringing thigh toward your shoulder
- this is a difficult exercise ... it may take some practice to coordinate your pelvic floor and abdominal contractions with the thigh motion

* same considerations as in exercise 2

6   **TrA & MF - single knee lift + bent knee fall out**

- maintain TrA & MF contraction while bringing one thigh toward your shoulder while the other thigh moves outward toward the floor ... again, it may take some practice to coordinate your abdominal work with the thigh movements

* same considerations as in exercise 2

Middle Layer Stabilization Exercises

Transversus Abdominis & Multifidus - Advanced Training

7   TrA & MF - single knee lift and opposite arm overhead reach

- sometimes known as the 'dying bug' exercise ...

- maintain TrA & MF contraction while raising one thigh and, at the same time, moving the opposite arm overhead toward floor; bring the arm and leg back to their start positions and release the TrA & MF contraction
- repeat with the opposite leg and arm

- not too difficult once you have mastered exercises 4 and 5

8   TrA & MF - double knee lift

- maintain TrA & MF contraction while lifting one leg up, then the other
- once both thighs are vertical, lower one leg then the other very slowly - concentrate on your TrA & MF

- for most people, the hard part with this exercise is maintaining a good TrA & MF contraction as you are about to initiate movement in the *second* leg
- focus on your TrA & MF contraction *not* the movement of the second leg

9   TrA & MF - single knee lift and opposite side leg extension

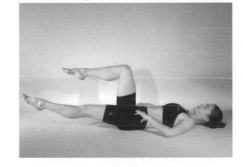

A very, very difficult exercise!

- many people find it very difficult to develop sufficient TrA & MF control to do this correctly and thus safely

- activate TrA & MF then raise one leg then the other as in exercise 8; once each thigh is vertical, extend one leg away from you, bring it back then lower each leg one at a time

Middle Layer Stabilization Exercises

Transversus Abdominis & Multifidus - Advanced Training

10   TrA & MF - double leg lowering

I hesitated about including this exercise because it is so incredibly demanding. Many people attempt this exercise but very few people - even elite athletes - can do this correctly and therefore safely.

• this exercise should therefore be done only on the advice of a physical therapist
• both legs are raised so that they point to the ceiling; the TrA and MF are then contracted and the legs lowered carefully and slowly toward the floor
• the legs should not be lowered beyond the point at which the TrA and MF contraction can be maintained without the lower back arching at all

Remember, if you are not maintaining control of your lower spine posture via a perfect TrA & MF contraction this exercise has significant potential to hurt your back!

Integrative Training - Static Middle Layer Exercises

The following is a lengthy list of middle layer exercises, both static and dynamic. A physical therapist can help you make appropriate choices from this list based on your present level of conditioning. Generally, most people will be working with two to six different middle layer exercises at any given time.

As with the previous exercises, if you have had low back pain in the past, maintain a consistent contraction in TrA & MF while holding these postures. If you have not had low back pain previously, the TrA & MF contraction is optional.

Initially try 5 - 10 repetitions, holding each for 5 - 10 seconds. As you get stronger, hold them longer (up to 30 or 45 seconds) but do fewer repetitions. Remember, correct technique is much more important than how long you can hold each posture or how many repetitions you can do. Never sacrifice quality for quantity.

1   **Back Bridge - wide base of support, four points of stable contact**

- establish a 'straight line' through your knee, hip and shoulder

- in general, all the back-lying bridges place more emphasis on posterior muscles of the body such as our hamstrings, gluteals erector spinae and latissimus

2   **Back Bridge - wide base of support, two points of stable contact**

- establish a 'straight line' through your knee, hip and shoulder

3   **Back Bridge - narrow base of support, two points of stable contact**

- establish a 'straight line' through your knee, hip and shoulder

- your feet should be closer together than in the previous two exercises, but not touching

- allowing your inner thighs to touch leads to use of the inner thigh muscles to help stabilize the posture - occasionally a therapist may want you to do this, but usually it is a method of 'cheating'

Integrative Training - Static Middle Layer Exercises

If you have had low back pain in the past, maintain a consistent contraction in transversus & multifidus while holding these postures. If you have not had low back pain previously, the TrA & MF contraction is optional.

4   Back Bridge - one point of stable contact

- maintain a 'straight line' through your knee, hip and shoulder
- this is much more difficult than exercise 3 as it demands greater balance and strength
- starting from the position of exercise 3, straighten one knee and hold; release down and repeat on the other side

- initially, you may develop some cramping in the back of your thigh since your buttocks and upper hamstrings must work in a shortened position to hold this posture ... usually a simple hamstring stretch before and after is enough to solve this problem

5   Back Bridge - two points of stable contact (feet on ball)

- maintain a 'straight line' through your knee, hip and shoulder
- note that the hands are on the floor again to provide a stability assist now that you're using a ball

- less strength required to maintain the posture than with exercise 4, but obviously a greater stability and balance challenge

6   Back Bridge - no points of stable contact (feet on ball)

- maintain a 'straight line' through your knee, hip and shoulder
- with the hands off the floor the trunk stability demand increases dramatically

- some people will move relatively quickly from exercise 5 to 6 while others will take longer to find their balance and trunk stability
- each time you add a level of stability challenge it becomes harder to maintain a good TrA & MF contraction - work diligently at this ... the TrA & MF will give you the sense of stability you need to perform these more advanced exercises

Integrative Training - Static Middle Layer Exercises

If you have had low back pain in the past, maintain a consistent contraction in transversus & multifidus while holding these postures. If you have not had low back pain previously, the TrA & MF contraction is optional.

7   Back Bridge - lying on ball, feet on floor;
     two points of stable contact, wide base of support

- maintain a 'straight line' through your knee, hip and shoulder
- this is usually less challenging than exercise 6

- to get into this position, begin by sitting on the ball as in the exercises on page 65, then walk your feet away from the ball as you lie back
- note that your head and neck should rest comfortably on the ball - do not allow your head to remain unsupported

8   Back Bridge - lying on ball, feet on floor;
     two points of stable contact, narrow base of support

- maintain that 'straight line' through your knee, hip and shoulder
- feet are closer together but not touching - keep the inner thighs apart too unless a therapist has instructed you to do so

9   Back Bridge - lying on ball, one foot on floor;
     one point of stable contact

- maintain that 'straight line' through your knee, hip and shoulder
- just as there was a big jump in difficulty from exercise 3 to 4, this exercise is much harder than exercise 8
- from the same start position as exercise 8, straighten one knee and hold; return to the start position and repeat, alternating legs

- ... add a hamstring stretch if neccessary

Integrative Training - Static Middle Layer Exercises

If you have had low back pain in the past, maintain a consistent contraction in transversus & multifidus while holding these postures. If you have not had low back pain previously, the TrA & MF contraction is optional.

10   Front Bridge - from knees, four points
      of stable contact

- maintain a 'straight line' through your knee, hip and shoulder *and neck*
- in general, all the front-lying bridges place more emphasis or demand on the anterior muscles such as the abdominals, hip flexors and hip adductors (inner thigh)
- the front-lying exercises also place great demand on the shoulder girdle muscles - you must have sufficient shoulder strength to do many of the more advanced versions
- performing the exercises correctly will develop strength in your shoulder stabilizers as well as your trunk

11   Front Bridge - from toes, wide base of
      support, four points of stable contact

- maintain a 'straight line' through your knee, hip and shoulder and neck

- recall that when beginning these 'static' or non-moving exercises, hold each for 5 to 10 seconds and work up to 10 repetitions
- when you can do 10, 10 second repetitions begin holding each repetition longer but do fewer of them
- eventually you will be holding each repetition for 20 to 45 seconds, but doing only 3 to 5 repetitions

12   Front Bridge - from toes, narrow base of
      support, four points of stable contact

- maintain a 'straight line' through your knee, hip and shoulder and neck

- same technique considerations as in exercise 11

Integrative Training - Static Middle Layer Exercises

If you have had low back pain in the past, maintain a consistent contraction in transversus & multifidus while holding these postures. If you have not had low back pain previously, the TrA & MF contraction is optional.

13   Front Bridge - from toes,
          three points of stable contact

- maintain a 'straight line' through your knee, hip and shoulder and neck

- focus on lifting the leg only a little using the glute muscles without any hinging in the lower spine; alternate legs

- usually much more demanding than exercises 11 or 12

14   Front Bridge Walkout -
          two points of stable contact, thighs on ball

- begin by kneeling on the floor with the ball resting against your abdomen - then roll onto the ball and walk your hands forward
- maintain a 'straight line' through your knee, hip and shoulder and neck

- the exercise is made more difficult by walking your hands further out and having the ball support you closer to your feet as in the next exercise

15   Front Bridge Walkout -
          two points of stable contact, feet on ball

- maintain a 'straight line' through your ankle, knee, hip, shoulder and neck

- as the unsupported length of your body increases, it becomes more difficult to keep TrA & MF activated correctly - pay close attention to this contraction as you progress into these more difficult exercises

Integrative Training - Static Middle Layer Exercises

If you have had low back pain in the past, maintain a consistent contraction in transversus & multifidus while holding these postures. If you have not had low back pain previously, the TrA & MF contraction is optional.

16   Front Bridge Walkout
          two points of stable contact, one foot on ball, lift other leg

- maintain a 'straight line' through your ankle, knee, hip, shoulder and neck
- lift one leg, hold, then lower; repeat with other leg

- quite difficult in terms of strength and balance
- these more advanced variations on the basic front bridge walkout can provide a great workout for the whole body but beware of the effect of muscle fatigue - stop when you feel your technique is suffering

17   Front Bridge Arms on Ball 1 -
          two knees on floor, arms on ball

- maintain a 'straight line' through your knee, hip, shoulder and neck

- exercises 17 - 18 are difficult primarily from a balance perspective and are thus effective deep and middle layer exercises

18   Front Bridge Arms on Ball 2 -
          one knee on floor, arms on ball

- very tricky to balance with this one!
- beginning in the start position for exercise 17, slowly lift one leg off the floor; hold while you balance on the ball and the single leg
- slowly lower the leg and repeat with the opposite leg

- again, these are also excellent for people who require improved stabilization of their shoulder girdle

Integrative Training - Static Middle Layer Exercises

If you have had low back pain in the past, maintain a consistent contraction in transversus & multifidus while holding these postures. If you have not had low back pain previously, the TrA & MF contraction is optional.

19   Front Bridge Arms on Ball 3
        two feet on floor, arms on ball

- maintain a 'straight line' through your ankle, knee, hip, shoulder and neck

- difficult in terms of balance and strength - a lack of shoulder girdle and trunk strength often limit people's ability to do this exercise

20   Front Bridge Arms on Ball 4
        one foot on floor, arms on ball

- maintain a 'straight line' through your ankle, knee, hip, shoulder and neck
- raise one leg, hold then lower slowly; repeat with opposite side

- our model has terrific shoulder girdle strength and a highly developed balance sense which she demonstrates here!

21   Side Bridge - from knees

- even in the side position, maintain that 'straight line' through your knee, hip, shoulder and neck
- you may either do several repetitions on the ame side or you might alternate sides

- these next exercises done in the side position target the lateral trunk muscles very effectively - expect some 'post-workout' muscle soreness the day after doing these for the first time
- these exercises require good shoulder strength

Integrative Training - Static Middle Layer Exercises

If you have had low back pain in the past, maintain a consistent contraction in transversus & multifidus while holding these postures. If you have not had low back pain previously, the TrA & MF contraction is optional.

22   Side Bridge - from feet

- even in the side position, maintain a 'straight line' through your knee, hip, shoulder and neck

- much more difficult than exercise 21

Note to Therapists:
- a good exercise to train the *transverse system* as per Diane Lee's /Andry Vleeming's 'Outer Unit'

24   Side Bridge - from feet, lift top leg

- a very difficult exercise!
- begin in the start position for exercise 23 then raise upper leg and hold; lower slowly, change sides and repeat

Note to Therapists:
- correct performance of this requires excellent activation and strength in the weightbearing-side gluteus medius
- as the upper hip is abducted, a greater demand is placed on the weightbearing gluteus medius to stabilize the pelvis

Integrative Training - Dynamic Middle Layer Exercises

If you have had back pain in the past, maintain TrA & MF contraction and slowly increase the number of repetitions of each exercise. You must have excellent control and the ability to hold most of the static middle layer exercises for 30 seconds before attempting these more difficult exercises.

NOTE: Start positions are on the left, finishing positions on the right.

1   Back Bridge Hamstring Curl
          • two points of stable contact; slowly curl knees toward chest & return to start position

2   Back Bridge Hamstring Curl
          • no point of stable contact; slowly curl knees toward chest & return to start position

3   'Dying Bug on a Ball'
          • one point of stable contact; slowly straighten one knee and opposite arm & return

Integrative Training - Dynamic Middle Layer Exercises

If you have had back pain in the past, maintain TrA & MF contraction and slowly increase the number of repetitions of each exercise. You must have excellent control and the ability to hold most of the static middle layer exercises for 30 seconds before attempting these more difficult exercises.

NOTE: Start positions are on the left, finishing positions on the right.

4   **Front Bridge Walkout & Leg Lift**
         • feet on ball, lift one leg off the ball then move it away from you and to the side (abduction)

5   **Front Bridge Walkout & Knees to Chest**
         • feet on ball then slowly bring knees toward chest

6   **Front Bridge Walkout & Pike**
         • feet on ball then slowly fold body at midsection, maintain straight legs

Integrative Training - Dynamic Middle Layer Exercises

If you have had back pain in the past, maintain TrA & MF contraction and slowly increase the number of repetitions of each exercise. You must have excellent control and the ability to hold most of the static middle layer exercises for 30 seconds before attempting these more difficult exercises.

NOTE: Start positions are on the left, finishing positions on the right.

7   Front Bridge Walkout and Trunk Twist
      • feet on ball; lift one leg, rotate body toward side of lifted leg - pelvis becomes vertical

CAUTION!
Dynamic middle layer exercise number 8 is a very demanding trunk and shoulder girdle exercise.

However, it may cause severe shoulder damage if performed incorrectly. Do not over-extend your forward lean or reach - your shoulders must remain bent and must never be in a straight line with your body.

People who have dislocated their shoulder in the past or who have shoulder instability should not attempt this exercise.

---

8   Front Bridge Arms on Ball
      • lean body forward on ball then roll ball away from body; pause, return to start and repeat

Integrative Training - Outer Layer Exercises

For most people the deep and middle layer exercises from page 65 to page 88 will provide a complete trunk or core workout. If you would like to include a few 'traditional' abdominal and back strengthening exercises these outer layer exercises are recommended. You should have at least a moderate degree of trunk stabilization and good skill with various static and dynamic middle layer exercises before using these exercises in your program.

1   Abdominal Crunches

- potentially hard on the neck and will not directly stabilize the spine
- having strong outer layer abdominals may allow TrA to be more effective at stabilizing the spine

- each of these are variations on the basic abdominal 'crunch' - the upper torso is lifted slightly with the hands supporting the neck and head

• may also be done on the ball with hands supporting your neck

2   Opposite Arm & Leg Lift

- conditions the large hip and back extensor muscles
- raise one leg and the opposite arm, pause, lower and alternate sides
- work slowly with a focus on control rather than speed

- *maintain contraction in TrA & MF while extending opposite arm and leg; keep spine and pelvis level without twisting*

Integrative Training - Outer Layer Exercises

3   Extensions

- requires a healthy back and good stabilization from the middle layers
- maintain contraction in TrA & MF
- lay face down on ball, with ball at or above waistline; raise trunk to the horizontal level and slowly lower

4   The Butt Buster

- maintain contraction in TrA & MF
- focus on movement at the hip and use middle layer muscles to prevent arching or 'hinging' in the lumbar region

- from the start position shown, the model's right thigh is lifted slightly; you may perform several repetitions on the same side or alternate sides

Chapter 8
Integrative Training: Sample Programs

The following are samples only. They are provided only to illustrate a rational progression from beginner to advanced Integrative Training programs. Your program should reflect your injury history, your stabilization ability and stage of recovery and the sport for which you wish to train. Always refer to the concepts discussed in chapter six when designing or progressing your program. If you have a back problem of any kind, a physiotherapist should be consulted to help you effectively rehabilitate muscles such as transversus and multifidus and then select the most effective (and safe) IT exercises.

Please note that not all IT exercises are intended to be performed on a daily basis. You might use one or two exercises from each group (deep, middle and outer layers) on Monday and Thursday and a different exercise or two from the same groups on Tuesday and Friday. Mix up your program every few days to keep things interesting and keep your body challenged. Appreciate that you will have days where the exercises will seem easy and well controlled and others where you will struggle. This is normal. Over a period of a few weeks you will notice significant changes both in terms of your ability to perform the exercises but, more importantly, how well you feel.

Beginner Level

If you have had low back pain in the past, maintain a TrA & MF contraction with all exercises.

Deep Layer Exercises

Single Leg Standing, eyes open

Ball Sitting, eyes open, with arm movement

Middle Layer Exercises

Basic TrA & MF activation

TrA & MF with bent knee fall out

Back Bridge - wide base of support, two points of stable contact

Front Bridge - from knees, four points of stable contact

Early Intermediate Level

If you have had low back pain in the past, maintain a TrA & MF contraction with all exercises.

Deep Layer Exercises

Single Leg Standing - eyes closed

Ball Sitting - eyes closed, one point of stable contact

Ball Sitting - eyes open, one point of stable contact, with arm movements

Middle Layer Exercises

TrA & MF with heel slide

TrA & MF with arms reaching overhead

Early Intermediate Level

If you have had low back pain in the past, maintain a TrA & MF contraction with all exercises.

Middle Layer Exercises (continued)

TrA with single knee lift

Back Bridge - narrow base of support, two points of contact

Back Bridge - two points of stable contact (feet on ball)

Front Bridge - from toes, narrow base of support, four points of stable contact

Front Bridge - from toes, three points of stable contact

Front Bridge Walkout - two points of stable contact, thighs on ball

Late Intermediate Level

If you have had low back pain in the past, maintain a TrA & MF contraction with all exercises.

Deep Layer Exercises

Ball Sitting - eyes closed, one point of stable contact

Ball Sitting - eyes closed, one point of stable contact, with arm movements

Ball Sitting - no points of stable contact

Middle Layer Exercises

Single knee lift and opposite side bent knee fall out

Single knee lift and opposite arm overhead reach (the 'dying bug' exercise)

Late Intermediate Level

If you have had low back pain in the past, maintain a TrA & MF contraction with all exercises.

Middle Layer Exercises (continued)

Double knee lift

Back Bridge - no points of stable contact

Back Bridge - lying on ball, feet on floor; two points of stable contact, wide base of support

Back Bridge - lying on ball, feet on floor; two points of stable contact, narrow base of support

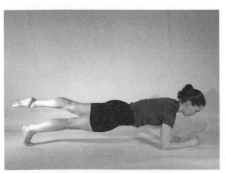

Front Bridge - from toes, three points of stable contact

Front Bridge Walkout - two points of stable contact, feet on ball

Late Intermediate Level

If you have had low back pain in the past, maintain a TrA & MF contraction with all exercises.

Middle Layer Exercises (continued)

Back Bridge Hamstring Curl

Front Bridge Walkout - with leg lift

Side Bridge - from knees

Outer Layer Exercises

Abdominal Crunches

The Butt Buster

Extensions

Advanced Level

If you have had low back pain in the past, maintain a TrA & MF contraction with all exercises.

Deep Layer Exercises

Ball Sitting - no point of stable contact, with arm movements

Ball Kneeling - no point of stable contact, eyes open

Ball Kneeling - no point of stable contact, eyes open, add arm movement

Middle Layer Exercises

Double knee lift

Single knee lift and opposite side leg extension

Advanced Level

If you have had low back pain in the past, maintain a TrA & MF contraction with all exercises.

Middle Layer Exercises (continued)

Side Bridge - from feet

Back Bridge Hamstring Curl

Back Bridge - single leg extension

Back Bridge 'Dying Bug'

Front Bridge Walkout with backward leg lift

Front Bridge, Arms on Ball 3

Advanced Level

If you have had low back pain in the past, maintain a TrA & MF contraction with all exercises.

Middle Layer Exercises (continued)

Front Walkout - Knees to Chest

Front Walkout - Pike

Outer Layer Exercises

Abdominal Crunches

Extensions

The Butt Buster

Olympic Level
If you have had low back pain in the past, maintain a TrA & MF contraction with all exercises.

Deep Layer Exercises

Ball Sitting - no point of stable contact

Ball Kneeling - no point of stable contact, add trunk movement

Ball Kneeling - no point of stable contact, eyes closed

Middle Layer Exercises

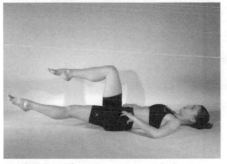

Single knee lift and opposite side leg extension

Double leg lowering

Olympic Level

If you have had low back pain in the past, maintain a TrA & MF contraction with all exercises.

Middle Layer Exercises (continued)

Front Bridge Arms on Ball 2 - one knee on floor, both arms on ball

Side Bridge - from feet, lift top leg

Back Bridge Hamstring Curl

Front Bridge Walkout Knees to Chest

Front Bridge Walkout Pike

Front Bridge Walkout Trunk Twist

Olympic Level

If you have had low back pain in the past, maintain a TrA & MF contraction with all exercises.

Outer Layer Exercises

Abdominal Crunches

Extensions

The Butt Buster

Chapter 9
Integrative Training and the Competitive Athlete

In the late 1950's and early 1960's, a Canadian physiologist, Hans Selye, developed what would become the single most important theory in sport conditioning science: The Specificity Principle of Training. This concept allowed sports conditioning specialists to design dramatically improved training programs for athletes of all kinds. Elegantly simple but truly fundamental to successful conditioning, the specificity principle states that *the human body will respond to any form of physical training in a highly predictable fashion*.

A person whose normal physical activity program includes four, eight to ten mile runs per week will develop specific physiological adaptations over a relatively short period of time which will increase their aerobic capacity; however, they will not experience any significant increase in their muscle mass or strength as this involves the anaerobic side of their physiology. Likewise, the person who performs three strength training sessions per week will increase their anaerobic capacity (i.e., strength) but only in the specific muscles which have been trained. The person will not realize a similar scale increase in their aerobic fitness, and their strength gains will occur only in the muscles which have been targeted during their training sessions. In other words, whatever the human body does on a regular basis is exactly what the body will become *better* at doing on a regular basis.

This simple fact of human physiology has made it possible for strength and conditioning coaches to virtually guarantee sport performance improvements using appropriately designed exercise programs. The person who trains in a manner specific to their sport will experience physiologic adaptations which will lead to improved sport performance - guaranteed. It has to happen this way because that is how our body works.

This means, for example, that the person who runs 3 to 5 times each week at a moderate pace but for progressively longer periods of time will become better at long distance running; however, the flip side of the specificity principle reminds us that the person who runs long and slow will *not* become any better at sprinting. Training long and slow does not train the body for short and fast. Again, *the body responds to training in a very predictable fashion*. Our body's physical performance abilities (that is our aerobic, anaerobic, flexibility, agility and balance capabilities) will develop and improve, but only if we perform exercises which challenge each in a directed manner.

In the decades following the development of the specificity principle, sports conditioning has matured significantly. World records continue to be shattered in a variety of events and sports such as hockey are played by athletes who are remarkably faster and stronger than even 15 years ago. While the training of athletes has become more sophisticated over the past 40 years, one aspect of performance conditioning had remained overlooked until very recently.

If we consider the techniques used by most athletes to develop strength in their core and limbs, we will see that a majority of recreational and competitive athletes still perform exercises designed to isolate a muscle group and train it separately from the rest of the body. The athlete will lay or sit on a bench of some form (which supports and stabilizes their trunk) as they perform exercises which target their biceps, hamstrings, chest, etc.

This approach to strength training developed out of the body-building culture where the single objective of training is to build enormous amounts of muscle mass. A body-builder isn't especially concerned with applying that increased muscle mass to some functional activity; instead, their interest is limited to the aesthetics of large muscles. The problem with this approach to athletic conditioning is that to some extent it fails the training specificity test. There is no sport known to man where the athlete uses individual, isolated muscles in the performance of their sport. Tennis, golf, running, swimming, gymnastics, skiing, rowing, paddling, basketball, volleyball - all sports require the body to function as a *linked system* of muscles and joints.

This linked system of muscles and joints provides us with an important mechanical advantage; the transfer of energy from one part of the body to another. Virtually all sports movements depend on an efficient transfer of energy between the lower body and upper body. Sprinters generate some of their acceleration via their upper limbs while baseball pitchers develop higher throwing speeds through the kinetic energy developed in their legs. The trunk of course is the middle link in the chain, the segment through which this shared energy must pass. If the trunk is not stable, some of this energy is lost, requiring the limbs to work harder resulting in less efficient movement.

Some conditioning coaches, usually those of national team or professional athletes, recognized this deficit and have incorporated exercises such as squats and dead-lifts into their athlete's training programs. These require the body to function in a more realistic manner in that multiple muscles and joints are used in the execution of the exercise.

While these are an improvement over exercises which isolate a single muscle, they do not attend to the issues of core stability and position sense. The athlete is often expected to perform challenging and potentially dangerous exercises without first having developed an adequate degree of spinal stabilization.

In response to these concerns, some coaches will state that the traditional approach to training works just fine. They point to the increasingly faster times attained by world class athletes as proof that current approaches are sufficient. These coaches are, in part, correct. Current techniques are vastly superior to those used 30 or 40 years ago; however, today's training techniques are not as well refined as they could be. They are 'sufficient' only so long as the majority of athletes are using the same approach, creating something of a level, albeit handicapped, playing field. As long as all athletes train this way, they are all exposed to the same relative deficit in training and no single athlete will experience a significant disadvantage. The fact that stabilization training is a new concept should not prevent us from exploiting its benefits to further improve upon today's sport conditioning methods.

Training muscles in isolation (or, at best, in functional groups) and without regard for core stability and position sense, will result in muscles which function in isolation and in athletes who have the capacity to produce significant power in their limbs but who lack sufficient spinal stabilization to apply that power safely and effectively.

A bench should be something you rest on between shifts ...

All sports require the athlete's body to function in some form of *stability challenged* circumstance. Soccer, lacrosse, baseball, golf, running (distance or sprinting), all require the athlete to stabilize their body from within, that is, to use their body's stabilizing muscles to support their trunk, hips and shoulders during the activity. Sports such as hockey, rugby, dance, figure skating, soccer and gymnastics place enormous stabilization demands on the core due to the rapid changes of direction and the stopping and starting inherent in the sport.

Skills such as swinging a baseball bat or a golf club, throwing a baseball or a football, performing a tumbling line in gymnastics, the accelerations involved in sprinting (either running, swimming or paddling) or the ability to absorb impact forces in hockey, rugby and basketball - all these create significant stabilization demands throughout the body. Even distance running requires the athlete's own muscles to support and stabilize their core over a single point of stable contact and a narrow base of support (their foot) approximately 180 times per minute.

Unfortunately, traditional strength training exercises are performed using a variety of artificial spinal stabilization aids - the benches and chairs which are designed to support or stabilize the athlete while they perform the exercise. These enable the athlete to isolate individual muscles as per the body-building approach to training. As discussed, there are drawbacks to this approach in that the athlete develops a somewhat unnatural form of strength, lacking coordination between core and limbs and lacking a well developed ability to stabilize the spine during activity.

The solution to this problem is quite simple: incorporate a degree of stability challenge into our traditional strength training exercises. By avoiding benches and chairs whenever possible the body is forced to create its own internal stabilization. Exercises that would normally have been done while standing with the feet shoulder width apart can be done standing on only one foot. Instead of using benches, sit, lay or lean on a burst-proof stability ball while doing any variety of 'traditional' strength exercises.

Making the transition from traditional to 'cutting edge' strength training

People who are just beginning a strength training program should begin training their core before training their arms and legs. In other words you should develop control in your deep and middle layers (as per chapters six, seven and eight) before moving to your outer layer. As your spinal stabilization skill develops then add any variety of outer layer exercises including traditional strength training exercises using machines such as Nautilus, Cybex, Keiser, or Atlantis.

Once you have developed good spinal stabilization skills and a moderate degree of outer layer strength via the machine-based exercises, it is time to begin learning how to use free weights. Having a qualified strength training specialist teach you correct and safe techniques when moving to free weights is a sound idea.

The final step is to combine your free weight and spinal stabilization training. This is accomplished by replacing benches and chairs with SwissBalls whenever possible. Initially, you may need to reduce the amount of weight used during the exercises as you incorporate the additional stabilization challenge into your exercise routine. This shouldn't be a concern in that, even though the amount of weight you're lifting may decrease somewhat, you are actually developing a greater degree of *functional* strength.

For those of you experienced with free weight training, continue as you have but begin working through the deep and middle layer exercises as presented in chapters six, seven and eight. Once you have developed good spinal stabilization skills and are comfortable doing at least the moderately challenging dynamic middle layer exercises, combine the two and replace your benches with SwissBalls. If you are a competitive athlete (and remember that even recreational athletes are often quite competitive) discuss the design of your program with a qualified strength training specialist. Remember that runners will need different strength programs than rowers, and gymnasts will need different programs than hockey players. The concept of stabilization-based strength training applies to all athletes but the actual program specifics will vary between different sports and between athletes.

Practical Tips:

Use a burst resistant ball for all your training.

All SwissBalls are not created equal. All have the potential to be punctured, some more easily than others. The key is to purchase a ball which will deflate slowly if it does develop a hole. Non burst-resistant balls can deflate in a split second, sending you crashing to the ground. If you happened to be doing an exercise involving free-weights you might be severely injured as the ball collapses. Expect to pay between $40.00 and $70.00 for a good quality, burst-resistant ball.

How big should the ball be?

This is not as cut and dry as some would have you believe. The common answer to this question is that the ball should be of the correct size to allow your hips and knees to be at 90 degree angles when you sit on the ball. This is important if you are going to use the ball primarily for sitting. If you are going to use it for a variety of exercises, the size issue becomes a little more cloudy.

For example, when laying on the ball to perform a bench press, your arms should remain unsupported at the bottom of the movement. Larger balls will be wide enough to support your arms at the bottom, making the exercise somewhat easier. On the other hand, larger balls will be best for exercises involving kneeling or even (yikes!) standing on the ball. The best answer to the size question probably involves trying different size balls for a variety of exercises and determining which size will best meet your needs. A further complicating factor is that for some reason, sizing can be variable from one manufacturer to the next (that is, a 55 cm ball made by company A might be the same size as a 65 cm ball made by company B). In fact, size can vary between models made by the same company. Be prepared to experiment and perhaps return a ball that doesn't suit your size needs.

How much should the ball be inflated?

Again this is not easily defined. Softer, less inflated balls will have a larger surface or contact area with the floor and thus will be less 'tippy'. This might be a good thing for novices or people with especially poor balance reactions. More experienced users often want the added instability that comes with a maximally inflated ball. You can also think about varying the inflation of your ball depending on your skill level with certain exercises. For example if you have just begun the dynamic middle layer exercises and are having difficulty maintaining your balance, you might want to deflate your ball a little, making it more stable. As you become more comfortable with the exercises, inflate the ball further which will make the exercises more challenging. Experienced users tend to prefer a very firm ball as it is more responsive and demanding from a control perspective.

How many repetitions should I do?

If you are doing the spinal stabilization exercises as in chapters six, seven and eight, then you should perform each exercise to the point of fatigue. By fatigue I mean *the point at which you can no longer perform the exercise with excellent technique.* If you are doing stabilization-based strength training exercises such as chest presses or single arm rowing using the ball as a bench, select the number of repetitions as you would with traditional strength training exercises (lower weights and higher repetitions for muscular endurance, heavier weights and lower repetitions for strength and power development). You must be able to complete the set using good technique and while maintaining excellent spinal stabilization.

The following is a selection of stabilization-based strength exercises to demonstrate the potential application of these ideas. Have fun and at all times, be safe!

Integrated Strength, Stability & Balance Training

chest press

chest 'fly'

bench press

military press

Integrated Strength, Stability & Balance Training

single arm row

push ups, from thighs

push ups, from feet

single arm triceps press

shoulder abduction - sitting on ball, 1 point of stable contact

shoulder abduction - kneeling on ball

seated bicep curl, 1 point of stable contact

kneeling bicep curl

ball on the wall squats

single leg ball squats

ball squats - use tricep dip rack for safety!

Chapter 10
Spinal Stabilization in Back Injury Prevention Programs

In 1997 our facility was approached by a local health care complex to develop a back injury prevention program for its staff. We looked at the available research into existing back injury prevention programs and found a substantial number of studies. The majority of the studies which evaluated the effectiveness of these programs came to the same conclusion: back injury prevention programs hadn't worked. It appeared that programs which taught basic back strengthening exercises and lifting techniques failed to reduce the number of injuries, the severity of injuries or the number of days people lost at work due to back injury.

With our current understanding of spinal function we can identify two primary problems which existed with these programs. The strengthening exercises did not train the correct muscles (especially the deep and middle layers) and the lifting styles which were taught were not techniques the workers could actually use in their real-life jobs.

The exercise approach used in these programs was not based on the research described in this book; therefore, like all exercise-based programs of that era, success was limited by a relatively poor understanding of spinal function. The muscles targeted were typically from the outer layer and, as we have outlined previously, these muscles are not designed to protect and support our spine.

A related issue involved the use of the 'pelvic tilt' in old-style back education programs. The pelvic tilt was often described as a good posture to work from; indeed, many abdominal and other exercises emphasized this flexed position of the lower back. Further, many people were taught to lift while maintaining a pelvic tilt. Research in the mid-1990's demonstrated that the posture of the typical pelvic tilt actually leads to a loss of stability in the lower spine, as opposed to an increase in strength.

For this reason, the pelvic tilt is no longer used by most physiotherapists, except with people who have very specific types of back problems which still benefit from this posture. In general, the pelvic tilt, both as an exercise and as a posture to work or exercise from, should be avoided. It is now understood that maintaining a neutral low back posture, i.e., maintaining the natural curve of your lower back, is a much better posture from which to work. This is true both for lifting and performing your core stabilization exercises.

A second problem with traditional back education/injury prevention programs centered on the ability for workers to actually use the lifting techniques taught to them. The lifting techniques taught on these courses were often not valid in the person's actual work environment. Clients have mentioned repeatedly that while they could easily perform a 'proper' lift in a practice situation, their ability to use these lifting styles on the job was minimal. Too often something about their work environment prevented them from using the 'ideal' style of lifting.

Examples of this are the night shift nurse who finds herself working alone instead of with a partner and putting 25 nursing home residents to bed without help; the long haul trucker who sits for ten hours behind the wheel, then has to unload a tightly packed truck without sufficient room to move about or lift correctly; the factory worker on an assembly line who performs the same repetitive body motion for two hours then needs to lift a single heavy item while rotating and bending forward.

In these circumstances, if the nurse, trucker or factory worker lacked the ability to stabilize their spine via their middle layer muscles, they would be exposed to an increased risk of spinal injury. Since these problems occur with regularity, and since our work environments can change suddenly and unpredictably, the only sensible solution is to recognize the need for people to have better functioning stabilization muscles. If injury prevention programs continue to rely on the use of 'correct' lifting technique, people will continue to sustain back injuries. People must develop better stabilized spines if we are to truly decrease injury rates.

Another problem which may have affected the success of these and other programs was the extent to which the person performed their exercises. The best injury prevention program in the world will obviously fail if the person does not do the exercises. In the case of the older-style exercise programs, it is possible that people sensed the lack of true benefit of the exercises and were therefore not especially motivated to continue. Similarly, people may have been 'put off' the overall program, including their exercises, due to an awareness that they would never be able to lift at work in the style they were being taught on the back education course.

The bottom line with work-related back injury is that most people with physically demanding jobs lack the necessary core stability to do their job safely. The physical demands of working and lifting all day overwhelm their back's ability to correctly stabilize itself, leaving them vulnerable to injury. While correct lifting technique is certainly important and should be used whenever possible, the reality is that a person will occasionally be unable to lift properly. It is at these times that they must have adequate stabilization to lessen their risk of injury.

For these reasons, successful back injury prevention programs will no doubt begin to borrow from the spinal stabilization exercise catalogue. Given that spinal stabilization is based upon a more sophisticated appreciation of spinal function than were the older programs, this approach will be of benefit to virtually anyone who has a spine. The progression of exercises developed in chapters five to eight may be used for back injury prevention programs, just as it can be used for people recovering from back injury.

Chapter 11
Spinal Stabilization Success Stories

Many back exercise programs have been promoted in the past and this is obviously not the first time a health care professional has suggested that a certain exercise program would be of significant benefit to people with low back pain. While I hope that the explanations and arguments I have presented in favour of the Australian spinal stabilization approach have been convincing, it is certainly reassuring to learn about others with similar problems who have benefited from this approach.

This section will introduce seven people who, like you, have been through some kind of back pain problem. I have selected their stories because they represent a range of ages and fitness levels as well as different types of back pain; some of them sustained an injury to their spine while some simply developed a painful back for no apparent reason. Some of these people are competitive athletes, most are not.

The common denominator tying these people together however was their motivation to get well. They worked diligently and carefully at their exercises. Despite busy lives and hectic schedules they set aside time each week and did their exercises regularly. They made an effort to do the exercises with excellent technique. Each one of them will tell you that learning the transversus abdominis and multifidus activation was difficult. Some people 'got it' in a few days, some took up to three or four weeks.

Despite the scheduling difficulties and the initial challenge of learning the transversus abdominis activation, they worked at their program. They no longer wanted to be limited by pain and they sensed the inherent logic in the design of the exercises. They recognized that this program was different; that *it made sense*.

Success Story 1

Bep Hardy-Mattern
- 40 years old; married with teenage children; teaches school
- enjoys walking for fitness
- many years of chronic low back pain with several unsuccessful attempts at rehabilitation

We were able to determine that Bep had an unstable sacroiliac joint. After years of joint instability and pain, her trunk muscles had virtually no idea of how to stabilize her low back and pelvis and she was in constant and severe pain. It was decided we would combine the use of a stabilizing belt designed for this injury as well as begin a trunk muscle stabilization program.

Bep's story ...

"It is very difficult to accept that your body is no longer doing what it is supposed to. After close to thirty years of competitive field hockey, three children and a very active lifestyle, I was dealing with chronic problems with my back. The process started while I was pregnant with my first baby fifteen years ago and tried to lift a box full of books. From then on, my back would 'go out' at the slightest wrong move, rendering me helpless for a few weeks.

"Physiotherapy was helpful in getting me back on my feet, but I was starting to develop a weakness in my pelvic area and pain in my hips while going for short walks. It was clear that more was going on, but it took four different physiotherapists, two doctors and a lot of frustration on my part, before it became clear that 'loose' sacroiliac joints, caused by a combination of heredity, competitive sports, three babies in five years and a very active lifestyle, were the cause of my pain.

"Since being diagnosed with hypermobile sacroiliac joints I have faithfully done my strengthening exercises. I have to wear a support belt (try to explain this to Canada Customs when you travel!) but I am able to walk without pain, ski and be involved in any low impact activity I choose. I have to be careful to pay attention to my body and not overdo it, but the targeted strengthening exercises have allowed me to live an active, pain-free life again.

"While there are days when it is difficult to make time for the strengthening program, pain is a great motivator, and after having dealt with all the problems, the commitment is only a minor inconvenience and it comes with a great pay-off. In the future I would like to be strong enough to live without the belt. In the meantime I will continue with my training program and will return to my physiotherapist every few months to update and progress my training program."

Bep Hardy-Mattern

Success Story 2

Bruce Miller
- 42 years old; married; works as an occupational therapy assistant
- enjoys fitness walks and bike riding to and from work each day
- several years chronic low back pain due to a spondylolithesis
  (see chapter 2)

Bruce's condition is a classic form of joint instability - his joint injury leads to a progressive weakening of the trunk stabilization muscles. As these muscles get weaker, his back pain worsens. Since pain can also weaken or *inhibit* stabilization muscles, as his pain got worse his stabilization muscles became more dysfunctional (the *faulty cylinder syndrome*).

Bruces's story ...

"My name is Bruce Miller and I had lower back pain along with pain and numbness that radiated down my right hip and leg. I had gained some weight and was frustrated with my physical condition. I was not able to walk around the block without having pain. I wanted to get back into shape so the first step that I took was to go see my doctor. He sent me for x-rays which showed that I had what is called a *spondylolisthesis*, a big word for the lower back pain I was having. My doctor suggested that I see a physiotherapist.

"After an initial assessment by the physiotherapist a treatment program was set up. This consisted of exercises to strengthen the muscles in my abdomen which connect around to my lower back and help to stabilize my lower back. When I was first given the exercises I did them for a while but did not do them on a regular basis. My back felt better but I stopped. After a couple of months I returned to the physiotherapist who assessed my back and again made the recommendation to do the stabilization exercises.

"This time, I was more committed to doing the exercises as recommended by the physiotherapist. I worked hard at the exercises and kept regular appointments with the physiotherapist to monitor my progress. After a couple of months of regular stabilization exercises I was becoming pain free. I had very little back discomfort and the hip and leg problems were almost gone.

"I am able to do regular activity, ride my bike to work and have even participated in a 'mini triathalon'. I believe that it was the performance of the specific exercises that helped me to be pain free. I continue to do the exercises and would encourage you to follow the recommended program - it really does work!"

Bruce Miller

Success Story 3

Debbie Ling
- 23 years old, recently married; works as an occupational therapist
- runs for fitness
- chronic non-specific low back pain

Debbie had a localized increase in spinal joint motion at a single level of her lower back, a hypermobility. Specifically, her 4th and 5th lumbar vertebrae were 'loose' into forward bending. There had been no history of injury or trauma; however, for reasons unknown, her lumbar spine was not doing a good job of stabilizing itself. When she came to see me initially she had been unable to run for several weeks due to low back pain and her back was beginning to bother her with other activities as well, including her work.

Debbie's story ...

"Due to the hypermobility of my L4 and L5 vertebrae, I was experiencing back pain, most significantly after running several days in a row. When I went to see Mr. Jemmett at Maritime Physiotherapy, I was introduced to the trunk stabilization program as a way to strengthen the muscles around my 'loose' vertebrae. It was a concept that was very easy to understand, thus making it easy to incorporate the exercise program into my daily activities.

"Foremost, I could feel changes in how my back and overall trunk felt within a few weeks of doing the transversus abdominis exercises and progressing to the dynamic middle layer exercises. When I began to run again, I noticed an increase in the amount of strength in my abdominal, oblique and lower back muscles. Since then, my back continues to feel stronger and I don't experience back pain after running, as long as I maintain my exercise routine. Presently, I do my trunk stabilization exercises once per day, five to seven days per week.

"In addition to the benefits I've noticed with my running, other activities such as my work, as well as other sports such as swimming have been more comfortable too."

Debbie Ling

Success Story 4

Anne-Marie Wong
- 35 years old, married with young children; homemaker
- former gymnast, but hadn't exercised regularly for several years
- chronic non-specific low back pain

Anne Marie's problem was a generalized increase in spinal motion, most likely due to her years of training as a gymnast. As a teenager training for her sport, her young spine became more and more mobile. This would have occurred as the spinal ligaments became progressively longer and longer, allowing more and more joint motion to occur. This excess joint motion allowed her to move into positions most of us would never even think of attempting. Once the ligaments of a joint become loose, either by injury or activities such as gymnastics, they tend to stay loose. Therefore by the age of 35 she had excess spinal joint motion, but poor trunk muscle function.

Anne Marie's story ...

"I had been suffering from increasingly chronic, non-specific back pain for approximately three years before I sought physiotherapy treatment. I had attributed my back pain to "getting old" but knew I should be exercising more. With my competitive rhythmic gymnastics background and its emphasis on range of motion far beyond the norm, I had assumed my problems were due to loss of flexibility. Thus I undertook a stretching program on my own. Needless to say, this did not alleviate my pain! I tried unsuccessfully to strengthen my abdominal muscles by performing 'crunch-type' exercises but would experience rather intense back pain. I knew I had to find help when even simple physical activities were causing me a great deal of discomfort.

"I experienced positive results with the trunk stabilization program almost immediately. I realized only after I began the program that my chronic pain had progressively been impacting on my life, both physically and emotionally. My back pain had been interfering with my sleep, which affected my mood and energy levels during the day. As my trunk strength improved it was as if a veil had been lifted. My pain level decreased dramatically as I progressed through the program. I began sleeping better, which in turn meant I had more energy during the day. I soon had the desire to begin an overall exercise program. I am now exercising regularly and feel better than I have in years. I have found the trunk stabilization exercise program to be extremely effective and the key component in resolving my back pain. The exercises are challenging as well as fun – not many exercise programs can make that claim! This program literally changed my life!"

Ann Marie Wong

Grabiner MD, Koh TJ, Miller GF; Fatigue rates of vastus medialis oblique and vastus lateralis during statis and dynamic knee extension. J Orthop Res 1991 (9) 3: 391 - 397

Greenough CG, Oliver CW, Jones APC; Assessment of Spinal Musculature Using Surface Electromyographic Color Mapping. Spine 1998 (23) 16: 1768 - 1774

Goh JC, Lee PY, Bose K; A cadaver study of the function of the oblique part of vastus medialis. J Bone Joint Surgery 1995 (77) 2: 225 - 231

Hides JA, Richardson CA, Jull GA; Multifidus Muscle Recovery is Not Automatic After Resolution of Acute, First-Episode Low Back Pain. Spine 1996 (21) 23: 2763 - 2769

Hides JA, Stokes MJ, Saide M, Jull GA Cooper DH; Evidence of Lumbar Multifidus Muscle Wasting Ipsilateral to Symptoms in Patients with Acute/Subacute Low Back Pain. Spine 1994 (19) 2: 165 - 172

Hides JA, Jull GA, Richardson CA; Long-term effects of specific stabilizing exercises for first-episode low back pain. Spine 2001 (26) 11: E243-248

Hodges PW, Gandevia SC, Richardson CA; Contractions of Specific Abdominal Muscles in Postural Tasks are Affected by Respiratory Maneuvers. J Applied Physiol 1997 (83) 3: 753 - 760

Hodges PW, Richardson CA; Feedforward contraction of transversus abdominis is not influenced by arm movement. Exp Brain Res 1997 (114): 362 - 370

Hodges PW, Butler JE, McKenzie DK, Gandevia SC; Contraction of the human diaphragm during rapid postural adjustments. J of Physiology 1997 (505) 2: 539 - 548

Hodges PW, Richardson CA; Inefficient Muscular Stabilization of the Lumbar Spine Associated with Low Back Pain. A Motor Control Evaluation of Transversus Abdominis. Spine 1996 (21) 22: 2640 - 2650

Hodges PW, Richardson CA; The Influence of isometric hip adduction on quadriceps femoris activity. Scand J Rehabil Med 1993 (25) 2: 57 - 62

Hubbard JK, Sampson HW, Elledge JR; Prevalence and morphology of the vastus medialis oblique muscle in human cadavers. Anat Rec 1997 (249) 1: 135 - 142

Hubbard JK, Sampson HW, Elledge JR; The vastus medialis oblique muscle and its relationship to patellofemoral joint deterioration in human cadavers. J Orthop Sports Phys Ther 1998 (28) 6: 384 - 391

Karst GM, Willett GM; Onset timing of electromyographic activity in the vastus medialis oblique and vastus lateralis muscles in subjects with and without patellofemoral pain syndrome. Phys Ther 1995 (75) 9: 813 - 823

Klein BJ, Radeki RT, Foris MP, Feil EI, Hickey ME; Bridging the Gap Between Science and Practice in Managing Low Back Pain. Spine 2000 (25) 6: 738 - 740

Lieb FJ, Perry J; Quadriceps Function. J Bone Joint Surg 1968 (50-A) 8: 1535 - 1548

Liggett, CA; The Swiss Ball: An Overview of Applications in Sports Medicine. J Manual Manip Ther 1999 (7) 4: 190 - 196

Luoto S, Aalto H, Taimela S, Hurri H, Pyykko I, Alaranta H; One-Footed and Externally Disturbed Two-Footed Postural Control in Patients With Chronic Low Back Pain and Healthy Control Subjects. Spine 1998 (23) 19: 2081 - 2090

Lutz GE, Palmitier RA, An KN Chao EY; Comparison of tibiofemoral joint forces during open-kinetic-chain and closed-kinetic-chain exercises. 1993 (75) 5: 732 - 739

Lotz, JC, Colliou OK, Chin JR, Duncan NA, Libenberg E; Compression-Induced Degeneration of the Intervertebral Disc: An in vivo Mouse Model and Finite Element Study. Spine 1998 (23) 23: 2493 - 2506

MacIntosh JE, Bogduk N; The Attachments of the Lumbar Erector Spinae. Spine 1991 (16) 7: 783 - 792

Mannion AF, Muntener M, Taimela S, Dvorak J; A Randomized Clinical Trial of Three Active Therapies for Chronic Low Back Pain. Spine 1999 (24) 23: 2435 - 2448

Massion J; Movement, Posture and Equilibrium: Interaction and Coordination. Progress in Neurobiol 1992 (38): 35 - 56

McGill SM; Low Back Exercises: Evidence for Improving Exercise Regimens. Phys Ther 1998 (78): 754 - 765

McGill SM: Kinetic Potential of the Lumbar Trunk Musculature About Three Orthogonal Orthopaedic Axes in Extreme Postures. Spine 1991 (16) 7: 809 - 815

McLain RF; Mechanoreceptor Endings in Human Cervical Facet Joints. Spine (1994 919) 5: 495 - 501

Michelson JD, Hutchins C, Mechanoreceptors in the human ankle ligaments. J Bone Joint Surgery 1995 (77) 2:219 - 224

Mirzabeigi E, Jordan C, Gronley JK, Rockowitz NL, Perry J; Isolation of the vastus medialis oblique muscle during exercise. Am J Sports Med 1999 (27) 1: 50 - 53

Mouchnino L, Aurenty R, Massion J, Pedotti A; Coordination Between Equilibrium and Head-Trunk Orientation During Leg Movement: A New Strategy Built Up by Training. J Neurophysiology 1992 (67) 6: 1587 - 1598

Okawa A, Shinomiya K, Komori H, Muneta T, Arai Y, Nakai O; Dynamic Motion Study of the Whole Lumbar Spine by Videofluoroscopy. Spine 1998 (23) 16: 1743 - 1749

O'Sullivan PB, Twomey LT, Allison GT; Evaluation of specific stabilizing exercise in the treatment of chronic low back pain with radiographic diagnosis of spondylolysis or spondylolisthesis. Spine 1997 (22) 24: 2959 - 2967

Oxland T, Panjabi MM; The Onset and Progression of Spinal Injury: A Demonstration of Neutral Zone Sensitivity. J Biomechanics 1992 (25) 10: 1165 - 1172

Panjabi MM, Kifune M, Liu W, Arand M, Vasavada A, Oxland TR; Graded thoracolumbar spinal injuries: development of multidirectional instability. Eur Spine J 1998 (7): 332 - 339

Panjabi MM; The Stabilizing System of the Spine. Part 1. Function, Dysfunction, Adaptation and Enhancement. J Spinal Disorders 1992 (5) 4: 383 - 389

Panjabi MM; The Stabilizing System of the Spine. Part 2. Neutral Zone and Instability Hypothesis. J Spinal Disorders 1992 (5) 4: 390 - 397

Panjabi MM; Experimental Determination of Spinal Motion Segment Behaviour. Ortho Clinics of North Am 1977 (8) 1: 169 - 180

Petrofsky JS, Phillips CA; Closed-loop control of movement of skeletal muscle. Crit Rev Biomed Eng 1985 (13) 1: 35 - 96

Pool-Goudzwaard AL, Vleeming A, Stoeckart R, Snijders CJ, Mens JMA; Insufficient lumbopelvic Stability: a clinical, anatomical and biomechanical approach to 'a-specific' low back pain. Manual Therapy 1998 (3) 1: 12 - 20

Quint U, Wilke HJ, Shirazi A, Parnianpour M, Loer F, Claes LE: Importance of the Intersegmental Trunk Muscles for the Stability of the Lumbar Spine. Spine 1998 (23) 18: 1937 - 1945

Radebold A, Cholewicki J, Panjabi MM, Patel TC; Muscle Response Pattern to Sudden Trunk Loading in Healthy Individuals and in Patients with Chronic Low Back Pain. Spine 2000 (25) 8: 947 - 954

Raimondo RA, Ahmad CS, Blankevoort L, April EW, Grelsamer RP, Henry JH; Patellar stabilization: a quantitative evaluation of the vastus medialis oblique muscle. Orthopedics 1998 (21) 7: 791 - 795

Rantanen J, Hurme M, Falck B, Alaranta H, Nykvist F, Lehto M, Einola S, Kalimo H; The Lumbar Multifidus Muscle Five Years After Surgery for a Lumbar Intervertebral Disc Herniation. Spine 1993 (18) 5: 568 - 574

Roberts S, Eisenstein SM, Menage J, Evans EH, Ashton IK; Mechanoreceptors in Intervertebral Discs. Morphology, distribution and Neuropeptides. Spine 1995 (20) 24: 2645 - 2651

Safran MR, Allen AA, Lephart SM, Borsa PA, Fu FH, Harner CD; Proprioception in the posterior cruciate ligament deficient knee. Knee Surg Sports Traumtol Arthrosc 1999 (7) 5: 310 - 317

Sato K, Kikuchi S, Yonezawa T; In Vivo Intradiscal Pressure Measurement in Healthy Individuals and in Patients With Ongoing Back Problems. Spine 1999 (24) 23: 2468 - 2474

Sheehy P, Burdett RG, Irrang JJ, VanSwearingen J; An electromyographic study of vastus medialis oblique and vastus lateralis activity while ascending and descending steps. J Orthop Sports Phys Ther 1998 (27) 6: 423 - 429

Solomonow M, Zhou B, Baratta RV, Lu Y, Harris M; Biomechanics of Increased Exposure to Lumbar Injury Caused by Cyclic Loading: Part 1. Loss of Reflexive Muscular Stabilization. Spine 1999 (24) 23: 2426 - 2434

Solomonow M, Zhou B, Harris M, Lu Y, Baratta RV; The Ligamento-Muscular Stabilizing System of the Spine. Spine 1998 (23) 23: 2552 - 2562

Solomonow M, Guanche C, Wink C, Knatt T, Baratta RV, Lu Y; Mechanoreceptors and reflex arc in the feline shoulder. J Shoulder Elbow Surg 1996 (5) 2: 139 - 146

Spencer JD, Hayes K, Alexander IJ; Knee Joint Effusion and Quadriceps Reflex Inhibition in Man. Arch Phys Med Rehabil 1984 (65): 171 - 177

Taimela S, Takala EP, Asklof T, Seppala K, Parviainen S; Active Treatment of Chronic Neck Pain. Spine 2000 (25) 8: 1021 - 1027

Valeriani M, Restuccia D, Di Lazzaro V, Franceschi F, Fabbriciani C, Tonali P; Clinical and Neurophysiological Abnormalities Before and After Reconstruction of the Anterior Cruciate Ligament of the Knee. Acta Neurol Scand 1999 (99) 5: 303 - 307

Vangsness CT, Ennis M, Taylor JG, Atkinson R; Neural Anatomy of the Glenohumeral Ligaments, Labrum and Subacromial Bursa. Arthroscopy 1995 (11) 2: 180 - 184

Vernazza-Martin S, Martin N, Cincera M, Pedotti A, Massion J; Arm raising in humans under loaded vs. unloaded and bipedal vs. unipedal conditions. Brain Research 1999 (846): 12 - 22

Vezina MJ, Hubley-Kozey CL, Egan DA; A Review of the Muscle Activation Patterns Associated with the Pelvic Tilt Exercise Used in the Treatment of Low Back Pain. J Manual Manip Ther 1998 (6) 4: 191 - 201

Wilke HJ, Wolf S, Claes LE, Arand M, Wiesend A; Stability Increase of the Lumbar Spine With Different Muscle Groups. Spine 1995 (20) 2: 192 - 198

Wolf SL, Segal RL, English AW; Task-Oriented EMG Activity Recorded from Partitions in Human Lateral Gastrocnemius Muscle. J Electromyography Kinesiology 1993 (3) 2: 87 - 94

Zakaria D, Harburn KL, Kramer JF; Preferntial activation of the vastus medialis oblique, vastus lateralis, and hip adductor muscles during isometric exercises in females. J Orthop Sports Phys Ther 1997 (26) 1: 23 - 28

Texts

Agur AMR, Ed; Grant's Atlas of Anatomy. Williams & Wilkins, 1991

Bogduk N; Clinical Anatomy of the Lumbar Spine and Sacrum, 3rd Ed. Churchill Livingstone, 1997

Hall CM, Brody LT; Therapeutic Exercise. Moving Toward Function. Lippincott Williams & Wilkins, 1999

Kapandji IA; The Physiology of the Joints, Vol 3. 2nd Ed. Churchill Livingstone 1974

Lee D; The Pelvic Girdle. An Approach to the Examination and Treatment of the Lumbo-Pelvic-Hip Region 2nd Ed. Churchill Livingstone, 1999

Lephart SM, Fu FH; Proprioception and Neuromuscular Control in Joint Stability. Human Kinetics, 2000

Lieber RL; Skeletal Muscle Structure and Function. Implications for Rehabilitation and Sports Medicine. Williams & Wilkins, 1992

McGill, S; Low Back Disorders. Human Kinetics, 2002

Moore KL; Clinically Oriented Anatomy 2nd Ed. Williams & Wilkins, 1985

Richardson CA, Jull GA, Hodges PW, Hides J; Therapeutic Exercise for Spinal Segmental Stabilization in Low Back Pain. Churchill Livingstone, 1999

Winter DA; Biomechanics and Motor Control of Human Movement. John Wiley and Sons, 1990